Political Science at the LSE

A History of the Department of Government, from the Webbs to COVID

Edited by
Cheryl Schonhardt-Bailey
and Gordon Bannerman

]u[

ubiquity press
London

Published by
Ubiquity Press Ltd.
Unit 322–323
Whitechapel Technology Centre
75 Whitechapel Road
London E1 1DU
www.ubiquitypress.com

First published 2021

Cover design by Mattin Delavar, Ubiquity Press
Cover images provided by LSE, used under CC-BY license
https://www.flickr.com/photos/lselibrary/collections/72157621932553336/

Print and digital versions typeset by Siliconchips Services Ltd.

ISBN (Paperback): 978-1-914481-04-8
ISBN (PDF): 978-1-914481-05-5
ISBN (EPUB): 978-1-914481-06-2
ISBN (Mobi): 978-1-914481-07-9

DOI: https://doi.org/10.5334/bcn

The full text of this book has been peer-reviewed to ensure high academic
standards. For full review policies, see http://www.ubiquitypress.com/

Suggested citation:
Schonhardt-Bailey, C. and Bannerman, G. (eds.) 2021. *Political Science at the LSE:
A History of the Department of Government, from the Webbs to COVID.*
London: Ubiquity Press. DOI: https://doi.org/10.5334/bcn. License: CC-BY-NC

To read the free, open access version of this
book online, visit https://doi.org/10.5334/bcn
or scan this QR code with your mobile device:

Contents

Images

About the Contributors

Cheryl Schonhardt-Bailey, Professor, Head of LSE Government Department and Fellow of the British Academy.

Gordon Bannerman, Political Historian and Professor, University of Guelph-Humber, Canada.

Daniel Skeffington, MSc (2020) Political Theory, LSE Department of Government.

Lukasz Kremky, BSc Politics and Philosophy (exp. 2022), LSE Department of Government.

Ebla Bohmer, BSc Politics and International Relations (2020), LSE Department of Government.

Hilke Gudel, PhD student, LSE Department of Government.

Sara Luxmoore, BSc Politics and Philosophy (2020), LSE Department of Government.

From left to right (top to bottom): Bannerman, Kremky, Schonhardt-Bailey, Skeffington, Luxmoore, Bohmer, and Gudel.

Introduction

The Department of Government— A Brief History

Gordon Bannerman, Daniel Skeffington and Cheryl Schonhardt-Bailey

Introduction

This volume represents the first ever History of the Government Department of the London School of Economics and Political Science (LSE). While histories of other departments, as well as a history of the School itself, have been written, the Department of Government has never explored its own past.[1] The volume coincides with and commemorates the 125th anniversary of the LSE, and as such aims to provide a comprehensive historical account of the Department since its emergence in 1895. However, we also hope that it inspires the many thousands of students, academics and interested followers with links to the LSE to engage with the roots of the institution. Through building a shared narrative among academics and students, the volume also seeks to help nurture and shape the unique identity of the Department within the School. Importantly, the volume represents the collective efforts of Government Department

---

[1] Dahrendorf 1995; Husbands 2018.

How to cite this book chapter:
Bannerman, G., Skeffington, D. and Schonhardt-Bailey, C. 2021. Introduction: The Department of Government—A Brief History. In: Schonhardt-Bailey, C. and Bannerman, G. (eds.) *Political Science at the LSE: A History of the Department of Government, from the Webbs to COVID*. Pp. 1–20. London: Ubiquity Press. DOI: https://doi.org/10.5334/bcn.a. License: CC-BY-NC

students and faculty, who—even during one of the most disrupted years in the history of the School—worked collaboratively to bring this volume to life.

In the first section of this volume, we trace the development of the Department, before assessing the contribution of individuals and the overall impact of the Department on the School, on academia and in the wider public policy space. Subsequent chapters show how the Department's growth was coterminous with the School. From an initial loose collection of lecturers and temporary staff, which was more akin to a 'community of scholars', the Government Department has become part of a university structure which is far more separated and self-contained than in previous decades. A much clearer departmental identity has emerged alongside greater professionalism—the latter a particularly important theme from the 1970s to the present day. Chapter 4 and the conclusion also raise wider questions about the future of political science at the School itself. Looking at the impact of Brexit, as well as of COVID-19, they reflect on the nature and practice of political science at the LSE, the challenges it faces and the paths it may take over the next few decades.

The volume assumes a chronological approach, with Chapter 1 assessing the early days of the School between 1895 and 1920, when the identity of the School and its respective departments[2] were still in embryonic form. Chapter 2 examines the period between 1921 and 1965, following the growth and maturation of this proto department under some of the great figures in the School's history: Harold Laski and Michael Oakeshott. Chapter 3 assesses the years between 1966 and 1989, an interim period heralding a new era in the Department, with a great change in personnel and an uptick in professionalism and specialisation. Chapter 4 covers the period from 1990 to the present day, detailing the continuing evolution of the Department into a modern, research-led institution, and the factors that helped create it.

As the chapters proceed, we identify several key themes. First, like other university departments in the United Kingdom, the Government Department has moved from an early era where one or possibly two prominent figures (men, in this case) largely dominated the ethos and direction of the Department, to one in which the Department is more identified by a number of scholars. Second, the periodisation captured by each chapter manages to highlight one or two 'dramas' (e.g. the birth of the LSE itself, the 'tussle' between two prominent figures—Harold Laski and subsequently Michael Oakeshott, the protests of

---

[2] The 'Government Department', as an entity, did not officially exist until 1962—as is the case for all LSE departments. For clarity in this work, mentions which refer to pre-1962 are designated with the lowercase 'department', or with the term 'proto department', while mentions to post-1962 are capitalised as 'Department'. This distinguishes the early collection of political scientists at the School from what later became the formal creation of the Department itself. It should be noted that histories of other LSE departments have not always drawn this clear distinction between their pre- and post-departmental incarnations (e.g. Bauer & Brighi 2003).

the 1960s and into Thatcherism, and the COVID-19 pandemic following years of professionalisation). Third, using a wider lens, the history of the Government Department is something of a microcosm for significant developments in Britain, namely the professionalisation of higher education, the centrality of London, the growing focus on Europe in the 1990s and early 2000s, and the challenges going forward, post COVID and post Brexit.

Throughout the volume, we seek to trace the Department's development, before assessing the contribution of individuals, and the overall impact and influence of the Department on the School, the wider academic community and the public policy space. The volume embraces archival research, especially in the earlier chapters, alongside an extensive series of interviews, especially useful for the later chapters. These interviews include current and former colleagues of long standing, as well as key individuals outside the Department, who have been connected closely with it in some way. We have also drawn from interviews with alumni, who provide a unique perspective on their time in the Department. These biographical details form a picture of the people who comprised the Government Department, as well as describing the culture and essence of education that characterised the Department over its history.

The volume also explores the environment in which the Department has grown, tracing its location on campus, while also locating the Department ideologically in the wider context of British and European politics. In so doing, it explores the contribution of Government Department academics to national and global debates, and academic scholarship more generally. Over time, the Department has become more varied in its curriculum and research, as its scholarship has become more diffuse. It has also become more international and comparative, in keeping with greater awareness of international politics, as well as reflecting the challenges and opportunities represented by globalisation. The School's particular appeal to international studies has also been a factor in encouraging a broader outlook.

The Department is fondly remembered by former students and academics and is acknowledged as making a multi-faceted contribution to the scholarship in the fields of political science and political theory, both in the United Kingdom and internationally. All of us who have worked on the volume have been struck by the unique nature of the Department in terms of its influence, impact and relevance over the duration of its existence. The lineage of the Department, like the School itself, is significant, revealing important strands in British political, social and economic history. In many ways, the Department has been groundbreaking, often leading as much as following opinion, and providing innovative and dynamic ideas into the sphere of civil and political society.

The Roots of the School

The LSE was founded in 1895, in the late Victorian era, a period of great fluidity in British politics and of social and economic change, when the effects and impact of the industrial society created throughout the 19th century continued

Figure 1: Sidney & Beatrice Webb, c. 1895; Credit: LSE Library.

to raise public policy problems. Concerned with achieving maximum equity and efficiency, the founders of the School, Sidney and Beatrice Webb, George Bernard Shaw and Graham Wallas, saw the LSE as a laboratory and training ground for a new technocratic society.[3]

While the Fabians saw the contemporary socialist movement as the most likely vehicle for collectivist politics and the socialist transformation of British society, they were not exclusively attached to one political party. Their philosophy of 'gradualism', that is, gradual economic and democratic reform, was the overall strategy, but the tactics were those of 'permeation', attempting to influence all political parties for the progressive advancement of British society.[4]

For the Webbs, the LSE was not a propaganda tool for socialism, but aimed at filling the gap in 'political and economic subjects' in the same way as the Ecole Libre des Sciences Politiques, Paris, and Columbia College, New York, since 'no similar provision has been made for these subjects in the United Kingdom'.[5] Webb even had a spat with George Bernard Shaw as to the nature and purpose of the LSE, not wanting the LSE to be a tool of socialist propaganda as Shaw did.[6] Webb was clear that the Fabians had to act in the world as they found it, and not how they wished it to be. As Anthony Howe suggests, the LSE was

---

[3] Dahrendorf 1995: 6–7.
[4] Dahrendorf 1995: 42.
[5] *The Times* 1895.
[6] Kedourie 1993: 59–60.

designed to make thinking people 'socialistic' by examining modern disciplines with contemporary public policy resonance.[7]

The School's first Director, William Hewins (1865–1931), proved to be a perfect partner in bringing Webb's vision of a 'school of economics' to fruition. Initially, Graham Wallas had been considered as an interim Director, but he declined the position.[8] By the time the LSE opened on 10 October 1895, Hewins had found accommodation, designed the syllabus, gathered influential support, published a Prospectus and recruited 200 students.[9]

The first Prospectus indicated that there was to be 'no differentiation against persons ... on the grounds of sex, religion, or economic or political views'.[10] Public lectures and classes were organised across nine subjects, supported by special classes organised as a three-year course of study, including a research course. The Prospectus explained the need for 'systematic training in economic and political science, and the promotion of original investigation and research'. The LSE aimed at proving its credentials in encouraging study of the economic and social sciences. It was also a centre for advanced research, with research scholarships and publications by staff and students planned. Those students attending public lectures were not being prepared for examination, or any kind of degree course, but the Prospectus suggested courses and lectures would be useful for those planning to take public examinations such as those for the Civil Service, Council of Legal Education, Institute of Bankers, Institute of Actuaries and London Chamber of Commerce.

The School was to have three terms: October to December and January to March, each 10 weeks, and April to July of 12 to 14 weeks, and no public lectures in the summer term. As many students were employed, lectures were delivered between 6pm and 9pm and daytime classes were repeated in the evening. The subject range, many of a commercial and business nature, and evening classes, added to the vocational feel of the School. Admittance to all or any lectures and classes and full membership of the School was £3 per annum (in 2020 prices, about £403). A single course of 20 lectures over two terms and accompanying classes cost 15 shillings. Shorter courses of lectures were charged at 5 shillings. The School would award scholarships to 'students of ability' to enable them to attend the School and undertake research.[11]

The School's origins left a mark on the type of institution the LSE became, influencing both the development and the nature of the School's teaching and scholarship. While deliberately taking a different approach to the ancient universities, in terms of valuing empiricism and in avoiding a classical curriculum, the School did share some of the attributes associated with them, especially in its recruitment of personnel.

---

[7] Howe 2020.
[8] Hayek 1946: 4; Donnelly 2015b.
[9] Donnelly 2015a.
[10] Donnelly 2015b.
[11] Donnelly 2015c.

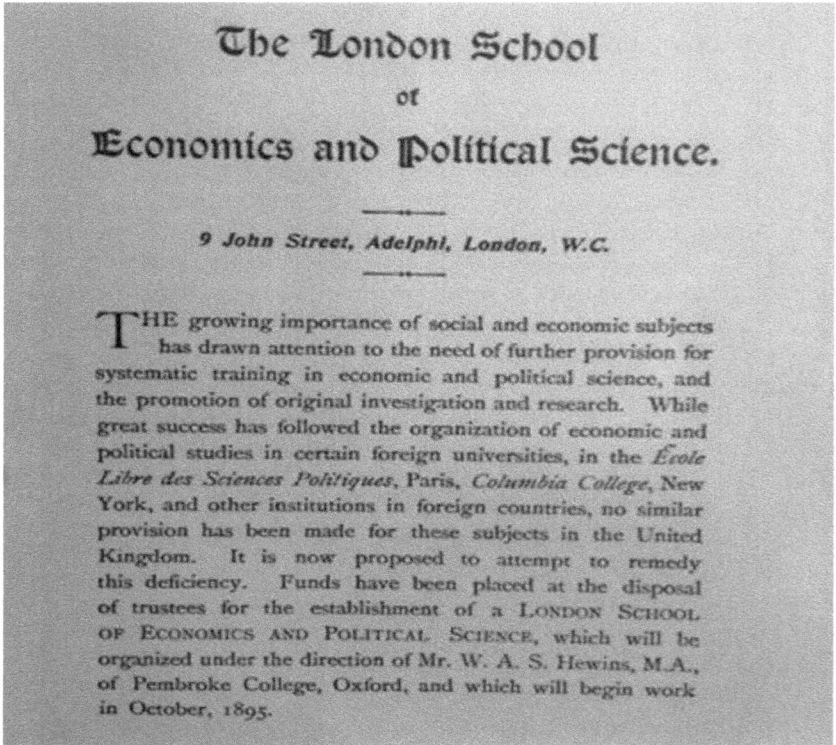

The London School
of
Economics and Political Science.

9 John Street, Adelphi, London, W.C.

THE growing importance of social and economic subjects has drawn attention to the need of further provision for systematic training in economic and political science, and the promotion of original investigation and research. While great success has followed the organization of economic and political studies in certain foreign universities, in the *École Libre des Sciences Politiques*, Paris, *Columbia College*, New York, and other institutions in foreign countries, no similar provision has been made for these subjects in the United Kingdom. It is now proposed to attempt to remedy this deficiency. Funds have been placed at the disposal of trustees for the establishment of a LONDON SCHOOL OF ECONOMICS AND POLITICAL SCIENCE, which will be organized under the direction of Mr. W. A. S. Hewins, M.A., of Pembroke College, Oxford, and which will begin work in October, 1895.

Figure 2: First page of the LSE Prospectus, 1895; Credit: LSE Library.

A Department of Government? Location and Identity

Where was the proto-Government Department located in the early days of the School? Several recent academics at the LSE have drawn a distinction between the informal notion of a Department before the 1960s and the more formal organisation thereafter. For ex-Director and official historian of the School, Ralf Dahrendorf, the notion of a government 'Department' was something of a misnomer, for at best it was 'small and institutionally almost non-existent'.[12] A formal departmental structure was not established until 1962. Before then, the 'Department' had a more nebulous quality. Michael Oakeshott was the first Convener of the Department, serving in that role (unofficially and officially) between 1950 and 1968.

---

[12] Dahrendorf 1995: 226.

Part of the identity of any academic community is proximity and location. Before the 1960s, scholars teaching Political Science and Public Administration were spread across the School, consistent with the notion of LSE as a 'community of scholars' rather than a series of isolated, self-sustaining departments. George Jones (former convenor of the Department) saw the informality of departments not having their own departmental co-locations as an asset and source of strength. For him, when departments became more developed, it damaged the School's 'inter-disciplinary cohesion'.[13]

The School itself was organised in a rudimentary way. All administrative tasks devolved on one woman, the erstwhile 'School Secretary' between 1897 and 1919, Christian Scipio Mactaggart. Such was her importance that on his arrival at the School, William Beveridge called the LSE a 'one woman show'. Miss Mactaggart was a key figure and point of contact between staff and students. She organised the afternoon tea hour, which Friedrich Hayek has claimed, almost certainly correctly, was one of the few opportunities the professors from across the School had to meet one another. That appears to have applied to those within as well as across different disciplines.[14]

It was almost certainly the case that, in the early years of the School at least, informal organisation arose not from any lofty ideals, but rather from shortage of space. Initially, the School was based in three sparsely furnished rooms at 9 John Street, Adelphi, near Charing Cross Station, with lectures delivered at the Society of Arts rooms in John Street, and Chamber of Commerce rooms at Botolph House, Eastcheap. The Society allowed free use of its halls in return for LSE offering courses in some subjects which the Society examined, including commercial geography and economics. In 1896, the School assumed a lease on 10 Adelphi Terrace, occupying part of the building inhabited by George Bernard Shaw and his wife Charlotte Payne-Townshend.[15]

The makeshift character of the School was superseded by the construction of the New Building, on the freehold land of Clare Market in 1900, presented by London County Council and opened in 1902 largely as a result of £10,000 and £5,000 donations from Passmore Edwards and Lord Rothschild respectively to equip a building for economic and commercial science for London University.[16] At the official opening of the 'handsome and convenient' building, Lord Rosebery as Chancellor of London University saw the School as 'a practical instalment of a new order of things'.[17] We can surmise that teaching occurred across the New Building after 1900. By moving to its new purpose-built

---

[13] Cook 2015.
[14] Donnelly 2016; Hayek 1946: 10–11.
[15] Donnelly 2015a.
[16] *The Times* 1899: 11.
[17] *The Times*, 30 May 1902, p. 9.

facility, the School was no longer dependent on the generosity of other institutions or the hazards of lease renewal. The poverty surrounding the New Building was plain to see, and worthy of press comment:

> The slums which surrounded it have only been in part removed; the works subsidiary to the great new street are long in the doing; and there still remain streets and courts filled with people whose notions of economics are primitive, being confined to the question of how to earn and spend their pound a week.[18]

In contrast, the New Building contained a luxurious range of facilities, including a reading room, large hall (with an approximate capacity of 200), administrative offices, six lecture and classrooms, a students' and lecturers' common room and cloakrooms, as well as space for a library.[19]

While these were great developments in the life of the School, there is no indication that the nascent department had become more formally organised, or that it inhabited a designated and clearly defined space. We know from the 1895 Calendar that Wallas's lectures on 'The English Constitution since 1832' were delivered at the Society of Arts rooms at 6.30pm. Classes for other courses were also held at John Street, Adelphi and the London Chamber of Commerce rooms, so perhaps all three locations were used for Political Science and Public Administration lectures.[20]

It is perfectly legitimate to ask whether a 'Government department' even existed before the 1960s. On the one hand, and a question not merely of nomenclature, the Department was never referenced in this way. Even though the subject matter of courses was progressively well-defined and became more precise over time, the Department remained somewhat amorphous. It is probably better to view the 'Department' as consisting of two streams of study and subjects: Political Science and Public Administration, the latter by far the most important.

Taken together, these subject areas did not quite add up to a department in the formal or modern sense. Partly that was to do with the embryonic departmental structure and a subject-driven curriculum, with a flexible interpretation of what exactly constituted 'Political Science' and 'Public Administration'. Perversely though, 'Political Science' was most often cited as the name of the department despite being the less important stream. Of course, the desire to advance political science as a discipline was important in this respect, but we should consider that desire to be more an aspiration than a reality for much of

---

[18] Ibid.; Sir Laurence Gomme suggested the new thoroughfares between Holborn and the Strand should be called Kingsway and Aldwych—names he found in old maps of the area, *The Times* 1916: 5.

[19] LSE 1901: 33–34.

[20] LSE 1895: 9.

the School's existence. The same may be said for other proto departments that were forming at this time. It is difficult to separate the development of distinct disciplines at the School from the histories of the departments themselves, for the former are invariably the raw substrate from which the latter emerge. As such, while scholars such as Bauer and Brighi have argued the International Relations Department can trace its emergence at the School as far back as 1927, the present work takes a different approach, by drawing a firmer distinction between the pre-1960s lowercase 'departments' or 'proto departments' and the post-1960s 'Departments' for clarity and ease of reference.[21]

While proto departmental structures existed in one form or another since the School's Constitutional Committee convened in 1937 to moot their formal creation, Departments in the modern sense formally emerged at the School in 1962. As the Calendars of the period show, before then the School was organised as a single faculty without organisational or residential division and evidenced by a single alphabetical listing of all faculty pre-1962. While many staff worked within broadly defined proto departments such as 'Government', 'International Relations' and 'Economics', their existence was still yet to be formally enforced.[22] The creation of departments as independent entities is conspicuous in the shift in the calendar entries to list faculty separately by each department, as well as naming the convenors of all departments. In Chapter 2, we discuss this more fully in the context of the Government Department.

The physical geography of the Department impacted the nature of relations between professors and the Department's position within the School. There were several problems in generating a departmental ethos. Location and administrative organisational structures were two of the most vital which were intimately connected. For many years, there was no departmental co-location, but academics were spread throughout the School buildings, where they rubbed shoulders with scholars from other departments.[23] While this encouraged a collegiate approach across the School, the absence of a precise location meant that a strong departmental identity was inhibited and difficult to forge.

Even when the Department began to coalesce, it was not without problems. When based at King's Chambers and Lincoln's Chambers, the buildings promoted a self-insulated sense of community somewhat separate from the rest of the LSE.[24] As indicated in Chapter 4, the buildings were somewhat shabby and run-down, and for all the charm they held for students and staff alike, they were no longer a feasible home for the Department by the end of the 20th century. From the late 1970s, when the LSE pursued a 'business model' instead of being a community of self-governing academics, the Department succeeded to its own location, finally ending up in the purpose-built Centre Building in 2019.

[21] Bauer & Brighi 2003.
[22] LSE 1962.
[23] Cook 2015.
[24] Dunleavy interview 2019.

Replacing the East Building, Clare Market, The Anchorage and St. Clements, and with its corporate feel and layout, the Centre Building could hardly be any more different from King's and Lincoln's Chambers, and is perhaps representative of the commercialisation process of the Government Department, and the School as a whole, over the last few decades.

Location has also influenced the nature and organisation of the Department in a more direct and immutable way—the influence which comes from being based in London. Influential seminars between civil servants and senior Government Department faculty have featured over the decades, with its proximity to power playing a key role in the success of these collaborative programmes. As Patrick Dunleavy argues, if the School had not been in London, its position, image and reputation, collectively or as particular departments, would have been quite different, and the student body would almost certainly be less international in complexion.[25]

The Development of Political Science at the LSE

Before the 1970s, the nascent Government Department was characterised by the domination of certain larger-than-life figures, from Graham Wallas between 1895 and 1920, Harold Laski from 1920 to 1950 and Michael Oakeshott from 1950 to 1968. Wallas and Laski were both influential in their respective contemporary socialist movements—Oakeshott, the diametric opposite, often seen as the prime proponent of a philosophical, at times quasi-libertarian, strain of conservatism. During Wallas's tenure, the School and department struggled to forge an identity, but with the Directorship of William Beveridge beginning in 1919 and the appointment of Harold Laski in 1920, a more clearly defined character began to emerge. With this character came a reputation—a reputation for radical socialist thought.

However, in the eyes of the influential political scientist and psephologist Robert McKenzie, this could hardly have been further from reality. To him, the School was a 'conservative institution in almost every sense of the term'. It was in no small measure owing to Laski that the School attained a 'wholly misleading reputation as a hotbed of socialism'.[26] Laski's role as Chairman of the National Executive of the Labour Party, and his prominence at the end of the Second World War, including outspoken run-ins with Churchill and Attlee, led to a perception that the so-called 'red professor' was 'soft' on communism.[27]

There was little in the way of 'modernisation' during the Laski period, tarnished as it was by the rigours of post-war reconstruction, the depression of the 1930s and the outbreak of war in 1939. However, Laski's position at the

---

[25] Ibid.
[26] Abse 1977: 97, 99.
[27] Ibid.: 8–9.

School was often considered in terms of a continuum of the School's traditions forged by Fabian doctrines of the Webbs and Wallas. Laski played an exceptionally important role during the Second World War when the LSE decamped to Cambridge, and the abiding memory of many students was that of great fondness and gratitude for Laski's way of making them think deeply about politics and political issues. Laski was valued in this way for his pedagogic skills rather than as a socialist propagandist—the latter often an accusation made against him in his forays into political life.[28]

His successor as effective head of the department, Michael Oakeshott, was quite a different character. A political philosopher and noted conservative, Oakeshott's arrival at the LSE was greeted with howls of protest from those concerned that the soul of the LSE was at risk.[29] Many protested vigorously against Oakeshott's appointment to Laski's position, including the prominent Labour politician Richard Crossman. This outrage by left-wing thinkers and politicians was not helped by Oakeshott's influential inaugural lecture, in which he paid tribute to Laski before presenting his own vision of political science. This vision was to prove every bit as influential as Laski's, shaping the Department well into the last decades of the 20th century.

During Oakeshott's tenure, an informal, unorthodox mode of administration was dominant. Likewise, academics often considered themselves part of a single-faculty school, no more so than when enjoying the congeniality and conviviality of the School's Senior Common Room, which acted as a locus for academics from different disciplines. As late as the early 1970s, several academics have testified to this Common Room remaining important as a lively place for political discussion. The idea of 'departments' was anathema to many scholars who opposed such formal, rigid boundaries in the School. This unusual structure was part of the LSE carving out its own identity, intellectual culture and pedagogic style.[30] It was perhaps befitting of an age which valued a somewhat casual, philosophical approach to higher education, unconstrained by contemporary managerialism or rigorous research standards.

Yet, while unorthodox methods of hiring and an aversion to new modes of thought or disciplines has tended to mark the Oakeshottian era as clubbish, and an 'old boys' club at that, it cannot be denied that Oakeshott's personal and academic reputation were both held in high regard. His dominance of the Department extended well beyond its intellectual parameters, encompassing the everyday life of the Department and its collegiate style. It was even Oakeshott's idea that the Department should have a Convenor and not a Head, that is, 'convening' colleagues and not based on top-down planning or dictation.[31] After his retirement in 1968, Oakeshott continued to be an occasional

---

[28] Ibid.: 57–60.
[29] O'Sullivan 2014: 471.
[30] Dahrendorf 1995: 209.
[31] Cook 2015.

presence at the School into the 1980s, remaining on some flagship courses such as his *History of Political Thought* seminar.

Towards the end of his tenure, and shown in Chapter 3, the School and Department were intimately connected with the student radicalism of the 1960s.[32] Other departments, such as Sociology and Law, were far more sympathetic to the students' cause. The protests were initially sparked by the appointment of Walter Adams as the School's Director, who had connections with Ian Smith's repressive regime in Rhodesia. As a result of the protests, the Old Building was occupied for eight days in March 1967. While there were issues specific to the LSE, campus unrest and student protests had occurred across the United Kingdom, including the new universities of Warwick and Hull. Drawing inspiration from events in France, unrest continued throughout 1968, and the School was forced to close in January and February 1969.

The impact on the School was multifaceted, transforming and in some cases embittering relations between departments and students, but also within departments. Within the Government Department, divisions solidified even after Oakeshott's departure in 1968. Oakeshott and Ken Minogue were particularly opposed to student protests, regarding them as juvenile and futile. A pervasive belief that the LSE was inherently left wing persisted, but the LSE was not a socialist institution by this point.

Reflecting on the School at that time, Rodney Barker has argued that the Department contained both left- and right-wing elements. Patrick Dunleavy's impression, however, is that the LSE was always on the right, and that the Government Department was 'very strongly on the Right' when he joined.[33] Perhaps the Department was reflecting a wider zeitgeist of impending change. The formation of the Institute of Policy Studies in 1974 and the 'New Right' coalescing behind Keith Joseph and Margaret Thatcher were indicative of a new challenge to the consensus politics which had held sway in Britain since 1945.[34] Among those in the Department who embraced this type of neo-conservatism were Maurice Cranston and Bill and Shirley Letwin, with the latter influential in the Centre of Policy Studies. Indeed, Thatcherite conservatism touched at various points with the older, non-political conservatism of Oakeshott.

The increasingly divisive politics of the 1970s was reflected in the life of the Department where there appeared to exist a Fabian left-wing group and a neo-monetarist Conservative group—though both were opposed to the left-wing student protests. Moving on from the student radicalism of the 1960s, there appeared to be more scope for channelling radicalism into more orthodox political forms, within political parties and pressure groups, rather than through direct action.

---

[32] Ibid.
[33] Barker interview 2020; Dunleavy interview 2019.
[34] Gamble & Wells 1989: 58.

Aside from ideological tone, the main developments to affect the Department were its refurbishment and modernisation of the syllabus, alongside an increasingly professional approach to research and publications. Both of these factors would prove central in forging the identity of the Department in the years that followed, creating the modern research-focused institution that exists today. In many ways, these changes were a response to external factors, with deep-seated changes in the fields of interest among political scientists, and a far more demanding set of objectives set by successive British governments for universities. However, the impression given by those in the Department at that time was not one of transformation, but rather of stagnation, or even decline. For the acerbic Bernard Crick, the School's glory days were long gone by the 1970s. He lamented that:

> 'And like our poor old country itself, the memory of unique power out-lives the reality … Yet it was a very tolerant and amusing place to have been in, both as a man and boy, and had the overwhelming advantage of being in London, the cultural and political capital, even if its great days both of scholarship and influence were plainly in the past. It is sim-ply that, like the ocean liners, the cinema organs, the cavalry and the Kibbutzim, it has had its finest days.'[35]

It was perhaps symptomatic of the recurrent economic crises of the 1970s and the sense of irrevocable decline that some could credibly write in this way. How-ever, much was to change after 1979, with the academic landscape transformed by the expansion of a more market-based approach to higher education. For most of the 20th century, universities had enjoyed considerable autonomy, and often seemed to constitute a world apart from the rest of British society. The idea of serving the nation, contributing towards a closer relationship with busi-ness, and forging a closer alignment between academia and the business com-munity was a constant theme in the Thatcherite Conservative Party from the mid-1970s onwards.

Ironically, the idea of universities serving the economy was one the School had subscribed to in its early years, as indicated in Chapter 1, albeit for dif-ferent reasons and under different circumstances, with the LSE acting as the handmaiden for many business-related courses. A stricter regime of Research Assessment Exercises, linking research activity to government funding, was established in 1986, later replaced by the Research Excellence Framework in 2014. Continuing the trend away from universities as secluded academic enclaves, university rankings or 'league tables', now a staple item in evaluat-ing universities, began in 1993. Fuelled by a rhetoric of shining the light of

---

[35] Abse 1977: 162.

transparency and accountability on universities, the new approach had a transformative effect on higher education in the United Kingdom.[36]

Research league tables, alongside similar reforms in the 1980s, created the pathway for a more professional Government Department. The Conservative Government's Education Reform Act of 1988 was designed to introduce greater efficiency and competition into higher education. The University Grants Commission was replaced by the University Funding Council to remove the prohibitive cost of expanding the number of students in higher education.[37] These educational reforms affected the LSE in a profound way. Research Assessment Exercises and Teaching Quality Assessments led to a more professional faculty alongside a more formal departmental structure and organisation. Within the Government Department, key appointments were made which had a transformative effect. In particular, the appointments of Christopher Hood and Brian Barry, both appointed to Chairs when George Jones was Convenor, were at least partly predicated on improving RAE scores. To boost the RAE metrics, it was necessary to publish academic works to raise the standing of the Department. The appointment of Patrick Dunleavy, a prodigious researcher and writer, contributed to this same goal.[38]

As outlined in Chapter 4, the appointments of Brian Barry and others were to prove a seminal influence in the Department's organisation from the late 1980s and early 1990s, overseeing a more efficient regime, especially relating to research and publication. A higher degree of professionalism, and adaptation of the business model of the School, has undoubtedly led to higher standards in teaching and research. An examination of political science departments according to the quantity and impact of publications in 63 leading political science journals over rolling five-year periods between 1993 and 2002 placed the LSE at number 41 between 1993 and 1997, rising to number 15 between 1998 and 2002. Clearly, professionalisation, funding and a commitment to research and publication was yielding positive results, according to this 'Rolling Global Top Fifty'.[39]

Yet, these positive and progressive developments also led to a more rigid view of what exactly constituted an academic, and the profile of academics changed somewhat. Despite clear improvements in many areas, there appears to be an undercurrent of regret that something of the foundational identity of the School and its respective departments has been lost in the process. Sometimes, this has taken the form of criticism of the new purpose-built offices and departmental space. However, the buildings are only the tangible outcome of what others had previously noted: the increasingly corporate and uniform nature of academia

---

[36] Jump 2013.
[37] Seldon & Collings 2000: 43–44.
[38] Cook 2015.
[39] The full range was as follows: 1993–1997 (41); 1994–1998 (39); 1995–1999 (37); 1996–2000 (37); 1997–2001 (25); 1998–2002 (15); see Hix 2004: 311.

which co-existed with professionalisation, league tables, research funding and performance reviews.

For others such as George Jones, Elie Kedourie and, most notably, Kenneth Minogue, this shift in tone and content represented a more deep-rooted malaise, and there was regret and some anger at the transition from the purer academic discipline and looser organisation of the Oakeshott era. Ideologically, there was particularly vehement opposition to the 'Third Way', policy-driven global economy ambitions and interests redolent of the Directorship of Anthony Giddens (1996–2003), and what this implied for universities and academic freedom.[40]

Academically, the Oakeshottian legacy had led to a curious perception in the Department that a qualitative emphasis in political studies was associated with the political right, while quantitative work became associated with those on the political left who wished to empirically identify, trace and measure inequality as a prelude and justification for reform. Here was one of the fault lines in the Department. Before the 1970s, the non-theory side to politics in the Department came under the general heading 'Political Studies', echoing Oakeshott's disdain for the term 'political science' that had been such a guiding feature of his tenure. The Calendars show GV100 was entitled *Introduction to Political Theory*, while GV101 (or its pre-1993 equivalent GV150) was entitled *Introduction to the Study of Politics/Political Studies*. This continued until GV101 was rebranded *Introduction to Political Science* in 2003. Simon Hix recalls how, in response to this, the quantitative and non-theory academics in the Department tried to consolidate during the latter years of the Oakeshottians, establishing a clearer role for themselves within the departmental structure.

The syllabus also changed to mirror structural changes in British society—the rise of Labour and the decline of Liberalism: the end of empire, the admission (and eventual departure) of the United Kingdom from the European Union. Most significant of all, we have witnessed the long-delayed arrival of political science as a discipline—at the School which included the discipline in its name, but rarely practised it.

These efforts to bring the Department more in line with political science in the United States also fuelled a change in the appointments system. The LSE calendar was aligned with the American appointments calendar to attract American applicants, as well as European ones. The Department also aimed to compete globally for staff, and this formed another major incentive for increasing competition in the appointments system, making the process fairer and less elitist in the hope of increasing the number of appointments of women and minorities.

Concerns were raised that the new appointments process would not support the appointment of more female and minority candidates, as the sociability element within the process would advantage more privileged and male candidates

---

[40] Jones 2013.

due to their affability. The worry was that the reformed system took the emphasis away from professional ability and more towards likeability.[41] This change was part of a wider process from 2010 onwards to professionalise the Department, aligning it with the international academic hiring process, both to attract the best candidates and to place LSE PhD students at better universities worldwide, but inevitably with great weight placed on North America and Europe.

Before the 1990s, the Department had little focus on Europe, and few European students. Patrick Dunleavy argues there was not a focus on European or comparative political science, but instead an 'Imperialist Public Administration' legacy when he joined, in 1979. This shift in concentration towards European expertise allowed the LSE to challenge the tendency to engage mostly with English and American literature, recruiting more academics from across Europe, and enabling the Department to broaden its scope and course offerings. However, the challenges posed by British withdrawal from the European Union places this broader outlook at risk.

The School's 125th anniversary also coincides with another historic event, one which any treatment of the Department cannot properly ignore. The COVID-19 pandemic has brought about changes to both the School and society not seen since the Second World War.[42] A pandemic of this magnitude has been faced only once in the history of the Department, back when it was still a loose collection of scholars led by Graham Wallas: the H1N1 Spanish Influenza pandemic of 1918. Its significance is usually overshadowed by the final months of the First World War. The war, which claimed almost 40 million lives, is rightly remembered as one of the most brutal conflicts of the modern age. An epoch-defining event for Britain and much of the world, the remembrance services and memorials which commemorate the First and Second World Wars—such as the Tomb of the Unknown Soldier and the Cenotaph—remain at the heart of British national identity. These traditions and structures have helped create and preserve a memory of the horrors endured, and horrors overcome, during these devastating conflicts and impress deeply on the collective psyche even today.

No comparable memorials exist for the victims of the Spanish Influenza pandemic, which claimed the lives of almost 10 million *more* people than the total number of military and civilian deaths during the course of the entire Great War, even given the most conservative estimates.[43] Most now place the total number of deaths between 50 and 100 million people globally in just two years, a quarter of a million of whom were British. And yet, while the wartime evacuation to Cambridge between 1939 and 1945 is recalled fondly in histories of the School, the pandemic of 1918 goes all but unmentioned, as it had done nationally before the outbreak of coronavirus in the last months of 2019.

---

[41] Phillips interview 2020.

[42] See Chapter 2, section entitled 'The Department and the War', this volume.

[43] Bayly 2020; More et al. 2020.

Questions naturally arise about the memory and identity that coronavirus will create in this generation, and of lessons not learned from the 'forgotten pandemic' of 1918 can be taught more effectively in the years to come. Yet, this also raises the question of the impact the Department itself has on the wider world. The Department has maintained a close connection to British political and social life since its earliest days, on both sides of the political spectrum. Laski's passionate advocacy on behalf of British Labour and socialist movements and Oakeshott's quiet influence on the roots of conservatism in the late 20th century are but the most obvious examples of a deep tradition of political engagement at the School. This volume begins to explore the deeper connections between the Department and the society it has helped shape and, in turn, been shaped by.

Looking forward, the Department faces the challenge of where to situate itself in a shifting academic and political landscape. British withdrawal from the European Union and coronavirus are both significant concerns for the Department and the School; challenges that will shape the new, European-focused research unit in the Government faculty, and define its future agenda. The conclusion of this volume—a personal reflection by the Department's current head, Professor Cheryl Schonhardt-Bailey—will explore these themes in more depth, situating the Department in the context of the times and providing some thoughts on the future direction of Government at the LSE.

Conclusion

When former Director Anthony Giddens hoped to restore what he perceived to be a 'golden age' to the School, he argued that the LSE had 'never been a partisan institution' at heart, but rather encompassed both Left and Right traditions for the common social good.[44] On balance, this seems to be the most accurate reading of both the School's history and the Government Department, which has contained scholars whose views span the political spectrum over the years. The Government Department at the LSE has long been thought of as a radical entity within an equally radical School, particularly among British elites; Anthony Eden was even said to have 'looked askance' when J. W. N. Watkins informed him he was from the LSE.[45] Yet, despite its Fabian origins, the 'red professor' Harold Laski, several intransigently right-wing Oakeshottians and the lasting perception of student radicalism, the School has perhaps fundamentally remained what Sidney Webb first intended it to be—a non-partisan institution, promoting rigorous social and economic research for the guidance of policymakers, in the pursuit of more efficient policymaking.

---

[44] Giddens & Pierson 1998: 49–50.
[45] Abse 1977: 68.

Moreover, while this history of the Government Department indicates there have been phases when the faculty has displayed a clear political orientation, whether on the left or on the right, it also shows a balance has been at work. Even during Oakeshott's heyday, the Department was leavened by a number of socialist scholars, and effectively split between a 'Fabian left-wing' and a 'Thatcherite before Thatcher' group.[46] The Department has appeared to 'move with the times', and in many ways has presented itself as a microcosm of wider political and social movements, both in higher education and in British society more generally. Its history reveals a Department in constant conflict with itself—conflicts between socialism and conservatism, qualitative and quantitative analysis, theory and practice—challenging and remoulding its very identity in dialogue with the prevailing attitudes of the day.

In an age of more rigorous academic standards, research-focused agendas and a shift from national to international concerns, this prevailing attitude has manifested itself in a drive towards European politics in the international order, reflected in the Department's syllabus, personnel and student body. Its strengths now appear broader than in previous years, with the rather insular focus on British politics eclipsed in favour of the seismic changes brought about by internationalism. In keeping with greater awareness of international politics, the Department has become more international and comparative over time, reflecting the challenges and opportunities represented by globalisation. Although interdisciplinary work of this type only truly began in the late 1990s, it has had a lasting impact, and this more global outlook and practice has brought the Department in step with the School as a whole.[47]

While the Department has come a long way since the days of its Fabian founders, several of their guiding principles remain central themes even today; principles promoting disinterested social, economic investigations and social research remain vital principles, instincts and objectives of the Department, as much as they have always been. This volume explores the history of these principles and values both inside and beyond the porous borders of the Aldwych campus; their evolution, adaptation and transformation, and the character of the Department they created through their incarnation, here at the London School of Economics and Political Science.

References

Abse, J (ed.) 1977 *My LSE*. London: Robson Books.
Bauer, H and **Brighi, E** 2003 *International relations at LSE: A history of 75 years*. London: Millennium Publishing Group.

---

[46] Cook 2015.
[47] Dunleavy interview 2019.

Bayly, M 2020 Fatalism and an absence of public grief: How British society dealt with the 1918 flu, 28 October. Available at https://blogs.lse.ac.uk/politics andpolicy/public-memory-1918-flu/.

Dahrendorf, R 1995 *LSE: A history of the London School of Economics and Political Science, 1895–1995*. Oxford: Oxford University Press.

Cook, C 2015 Tales from Houghton Street: an oral history. George Jones, interviewed by Clara Cook, 22 July. Available at https://digital.library.lse.ac.uk /objects/lse:kub826huw.

Donnelly, S 2015a Adelphi days—LSE's first home, 14 October. Available at https://blogs.lse.ac.uk/lsehistory/2015/10/14/adelphi-days-lses-first-home/.

Donnelly, S 2015b LSE's first Director—William Hewins, 21 October. Available at https://blogs.lse.ac.uk/lsehistory/2015/10/21/lses-first-director-william -hewins/.

Donnelly, S 2015c LSE's first prospectus, 7 October. Available at https://blogs .lse.ac.uk/lsehistory/2015/10/07/lses-first-prospectus/.

Donnelly, S 2016 LSE's 'Deputy director, hostess, accountant, and lady of all work'—Christian Scipio Mactaggart, 1861–1943, LSE History: Telling the story of LSE, 1 March. Available at https://blogs.lse.ac.uk/lsehistory /2016/03/01/lses-deputy-director-hostess-accountant-and-lady-of-all -work-christian-scipio-mactaggart-1861–1943/.

Kedourie, E 1993 The British universities under duress: Two essays by Elie Kedourie. *Minerva*, 31(1): 56–105.

Franco, P 2004 *Michael Oakeshott: An introduction*. New Haven, CT and London: Yale University Press.

Gamble, A and Wells, C (eds) 1989 *Thatcher's law*. Cardiff: GPC Books.

Giddens, A and Pierson, C 1998 *Conversations with Anthony Giddens: Making sense of modernity*. Stanford, CA: Stanford University Press.

Hayek, F A 1946 The London School of Economics, 1895–1945. *Economica*, 13(49): 1–31.

Hix, S 2004 A global ranking of Political Science Departments. *Political Studies Review*, 2: 293–313.

Husbands, C T 2018 *Sociology at the London School of Economics and Political Science, 1904–2015: Sound and fury*. Basingstoke: Palgrave Macmillan.

Jones, D M 2013 'The Conservative mind of Ken Minogue, *Quadrant Online*, 1 September. Available at https://quadrant.org.au/magazine/2013/09/the -conservative-mind-of-kenneth-minogue/.

Jump, P 2013 Evolution of the REF, *Times Higher Education*, 13 October. Available at https://www.timeshighereducation.com/features/evolution-of-the -ref/2008100.article.

LSE 1895 *The London School of Economics and Political Science, University of London, Calendar, 1895*. London: London School of Economics and Political Science.

LSE 1901 *The London School of Economics and Political Science, University of London, sessional programme, 1901–02*. London: London School of Economics and Political Science.

LSE 1962 *The London School of Economics and Political Science, University of London, Calendar for the sixty-eighth session, 1962–1963*. London: London School of Economics and Political Science.

Minogue, K 2002 Michael Oakeshott as a character. *Society*, 39: 66–70.

More, A F, Loveluck, C P, Clifford, H, Handley, M J, Korotkikh, E V, Kurbatov, A V et al. 2020 The impact of a six-year climate anomaly on the 'Spanish flu' pandemic and WWI. *GeoHealth*, 4.: 1–8

llivan, L 2014 Michael Oakeshott and the Left. *Journal of the History of Ideas*, 75(3): 471–492.

Seldon, A and **Collings, D** 2000 *Britain under Thatcher*. London: Longman.

The Times 1895 London School of Economics. 10 June, p. 6.

The Times 1899 The new London university. 1 May.

The Times 1916 A great Londoner. 25 February.

Interviews

Barker, Rodney, interview by Hilke Gudel, 10 February 2020.

Dunleavy, Patrick, interview by Cheryl Schonhardt-Bailey, 6 December 2019.

Howe, Anthony, telephone interview with Hilke Gudel, 11 May 2020.

Phillips, Anne, telephone interview by Hilke Gudel, 23 March 2020.

CHAPTER 1

The Early Years

A Department in the Making, 1895–1920

Gordon Bannerman

Political Science: The Historical Context

A key element in the pedagogic outlook of Graham Wallas and the Webbs for the LSE was that academic study should have contemporary relevance and application. Sidney Webb and Wallas both had practical experience of education and local government, with Webb a member for Deptford of the London County Council (LCC) and acting as Chairman of its Technical Education Board (TEB). He had previously lectured in political economy at City of London College and the Working Men's College. Similarly, Wallas had long years of experience on the LCC and the London School Board. Both wished to extend educational opportunities, and to this end, along with the LSE's first Director, William Hewins, though separately, embraced the merito-cratic aspects of the University Extension movement.[1]

It has been credibly claimed that the founding of the LSE owed as much to the City of London as it did to the Fabian Society. Several strands came together to promote the notion of commercial education. In 1888, the London Chamber of Commerce instituted a scheme of commercial education. Meanwhile, the

---

[1] Qualter 1980: 12; *The Times* 1947: 6.

How to cite this book chapter:
Bannerman, G. 2021. The Early Years: A Department in the Making, 1895–1920.
In: Schonhardt-Bailey, C. and Bannerman, G. (eds.) *Political Science at the LSE: A History of the Department of Government, from the Webbs to COVID.* Pp. 21–52.
London: Ubiquity Press. DOI: https://doi.org/10.5334/bcn.b. License: CC-BY-NC

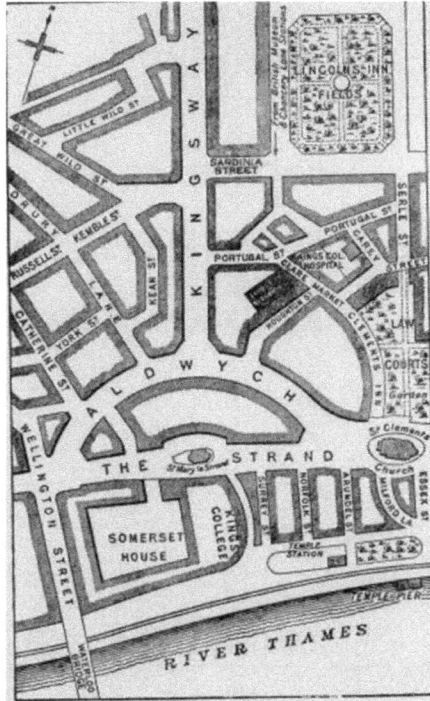

Figure 3: Map of the School, 1914–1915; Credit: LSE Library.

1889 Education Act led to the founding of the TEB of the LCC to manage funds allocated to county councils for the provision of technical education. The TEB was chaired by Sidney Webb until 1898, and as Webb also chaired, from 1901, the LSE's Board of Governors, he was in a strategically important and informed position. Both the London Chamber of Commerce and LCC helped establish the School on a firm financial footing. The LCC provided funds to the School in its early years, while the London Chamber of Commerce advertised the first session of LSE courses as an extension of its own educational activities.[2]

Theoretical rigour underpinned Webb's scientific approach to solving the problems of modern industry and society. Webb held the modernist position that informed policy analysis would lead to good policymaking—and that universities had a vital role to play in this process. Writing in 1889, he argued that the traditional elitism of universities had suppressed any instinct for political action:

> The radical vice of University life—the divorce of thought from action—
> has tended to deprive many resident University men, of all capacity, for

---

[2] Kadish 1993: 227–233.

real political work in national matters, whilst their social and municipal surroundings, far removed from the pressing industrial problems of
the great cities, tend to hypnotize their mind and to lull even the most
advanced of them to a placid acquiescence in, or merely spasmodic protest against, the *status quo*.[3]

For Webb, the divergence between thought and action led to a chasm between
the seminar room and the corridors of power. The Fabians hoped to bridge that
gap, and the School's early years were characterised by a dynamic, assertive
approach to academia, with public policy objectives never far from the surface. Universities in late Victorian Britain were not renowned as either agents
of professional research or social change. Political science had been taught at
Cambridge since the 1870s, with two papers, both largely historical, offered as
part of the History Tripos—a Chair was not established until 1926. At Oxford,
politics courses were taken in the History School within the 'Modern Greats'
or Philosophy, Politics and Economics (PPE) course of study, which was not
established until 1920.[4] Politics and Government, broadly defined, was a low
priority, and while taught at Oxford, Cambridge and the LSE, it was not until
the 1950s that political science in Britain acquired the trappings of an academic
discipline, with a professional association (the Political Studies Association)
formed in 1950 and a journal (*Political Studies*) published in 1953.[5]

Conversely, in the United States, the American Political Science Association had been formed in 1903, representing a new departure in political science methods and techniques, with the discipline concerned with establishing
the principles and practices of better governance. A professional journal, the
American Political Science Review, followed shortly afterwards, with its first
publication in 1906.

For critics of public school and university education, the main indictment
against it was its failure to stimulate the intellect and to connect academic
thought and political action. Having attended Shrewsbury and Christ Church,
Oxford, before working as a Classics schoolmaster, Wallas understood the
shortcomings of the ancient schools and universities. Immersed in ancient
Greek thought, Wallas embraced Aristotle's vision of the virtuous society as in
the *polis*.[6] He described what the study of government looked like in Oxford
in the late 19th century:

If any one [*sic*] had reflected that Government is a service like any other
service, and had gone to Oxford, for instance, which believed itself to
be a University given to the study of Government, and asked for advice,

---

[3] Webb 1889: 42.
[4] Hayek 1946: 1; Den Otter 2007: 39.
[5] Kavanagh 2007: 97.
[6] Qualter 1980: 4–5; Bevir 1997: 288.

he would have been advised to read a very few interesting books by Aristotle or Hobbes, but would have found it very difficult to apply what he read in those books to the actual problems of how you should administer a Factory Act, how you should develop Poor Relief, or what you should do about the gold standard.[7]

With a curriculum blending Public Administration, political history, constitutional law and the history of political thought, the LSE clearly 'intended to abandon the traditional Oxford and Cambridge approach to higher education'.[8] The *New Age* of 22 September 1898 lauded the School's approach: 'To the students of facts whose gospel is the blue-book, and to whom statistics are the sword of progressive faith, the London School of Economics is a very temple of light'.[9]

Yet, by and large, despite the language of innovation and the application of scientific techniques, much remained familiar. Most of the scholars at the LSE before 1920 were children of the mid-to-late Victorian period, where the dominant political view was shaped by the Whig interpretation of history, of constitutional progress and development. By the end of the 19th century, that interpretation had been transformed into the 'Westminster model' approach, presenting the political system of parliamentary sovereignty, elections, the party system and party majorities as the model of government, not only to be studied, but to be emulated.[10] It has been convincingly argued that this hybrid 'Whig/Westminster' constitutional model had a specific political role, as 'a means of inducting would-be rulers into a political tradition and an appreciation of the wisdom embedded in British political institutions and culture'.[11]

While the consideration for political science among the founders of the School extended to it being conjoined with economics in the School's name, it is ironic that modern political science never took a hold at the School; establishing political science as a discipline was problematic.[12] Anthony Howe has suggested a reason for this omission:

> The reason why political science didn't take off is that training for politicians in the UK was still much more linked to the arts and humanities than it was to the social scientific mission. Look at how political science was taught at the LSE. There were three key people. Wallas until the 1920s, then Laski takes over, then Oakeshott. But Wallas, although

---

[7] Cited in Qualter 1980: 5.
[8] Kadish 1993: 237.
[9] Cited in ibid.: 241.
[10] Kavanagh 2007: 98–99.
[11] Ibid.: 103.
[12] Dahrendorf 1995: 226; Hayek 1946: 7.

Figure 4: Graham Wallas, c. 1920s; Credit: LSE Library.

> I think he started off more interested in creating that science, ended up
> more of a political psychologist.[13]

Indeed, while Wallas was an enthusiastic supporter of the scientific investigation of government and political institutions, it was clearly the case that he was
not a political scientist in the more rigorous sense of the term apparent today,
but rather a public moralist who believed political theorists should examine
diverse fields of inquiry in addressing political and societal problems.[14]

It was undoubtedly the case that Political Science and Public Administration,
the two streams within 'political science' taught at the School, were intended to
promote an understanding of government, the policymaking process and the
historical evolution of local, national and imperial government institutions. The
fundamental objectives were differentiated from the pervasive political philosophy taught at Oxbridge. Early teaching was dominated by Public Administration and 'what do bureaucrats really need to know' with 'key experts' appointed
as lecturers.[15] The curriculum was probably closer to Oxford and Cambridge

---

[13] Howe interview 2020.
[14] Qualter 1980: 13; Bevir 1997: 284.
[15] Howe interview 2020.

than the Webbs would have wished, and indeed Beatrice Webb noted in her diary that Leonard Hobhouse was recruiting for the LSE at Oxford, while 'the young Trevelyans', presumably George Macaulay Trevelyan and Robert Calverley Trevelyan, were similarly engaged at Cambridge.[16]

With the cultivation of these direct links to Oxbridge in mind, it is especially notable to consider Goldsworthy Lowes Dickinson, who taught the same Political Science courses and delivered the same lectures at the LSE as he did at Cambridge.[17] Those courses were as follows:

- The Machinery of Administration in England;
- The Use of Political Terms;
- The Bases of Political Obligation;
- The Structure of the Modern State;
- Popular Government;
- The British Empire and Other Composite States;
- Some Theories on the Basis of Political Obligation;
- The Government of the British Empire;
- The Structure of the Modern State;
- The Functions of the Modern State;
- The Central Government of England comparatively treated;
- then in 1902, 'the most noteworthy of his courses':
- The History of Political Ideas, repeated with 'constant changes'.[18]

There is perhaps no clearer example of the limits to establishing a new direction in academic studies than this resort to a pre-existing curriculum. While the LSE assumed and promoted an empirical approach to research and teaching, useful for politicians and administrators, there was little methodological self-consciousness or construction of grand themes of politics and political ideas. The nebulous character of political science at the School was apparent in the almost complete absence of quantitative methods. The historical tradition was a key factor, for political science in Britain was inductive, reflective and largely non-theoretical—a product of the non-scientific approach of the 'Whig/ Westminster' model.[19]

The idea of a 'discipline' of political science has been characterised as giving a 'false coherence' to political studies at the end of the 19th century—a century increasingly dominated by a Whiggish interpretation of history, emphasising the progress of liberty, freedom and representative government, fostered by an intimate connection between history and political studies. At Cambridge,

---

[16] *BW Diaries*, vol. 16: 18/1421.

[17] Martin 2004.

[18] Forster 1934: 96–97; Lowes Dickinson returned in 1924 to present the course 'The Causes of the War of 1914', preparatory to his book *The International Anarchy, 1904–1914* (see Lowes Dickinson 1926).

[19] Kavanagh 2007: 103–104.

political science was closely connected with history, while at Oxford the great historian E. A. Freeman expressed this connection with the aphorism: 'History is Past Politics; Politics is Present History'. While that linkage was contested, not least by Wallas, 'historical-mindedness' featured prominently in the LSE Political Science curriculum.[20]

The grand narrative of Whig historians—continuity, freedom and peaceful development—was, however, overtaken by a more ethical and empirical, and less speculative, philosophical analysis of political studies.[21] The Webbs, Edwin Cannan, and Wallas were key figures in the emergent empirical and neo-positivist approach, with, for example, the Webbs' studies of local government and trade unionism intended to frame contemporary dilemmas in historical perspective.[22] As one historian has pointed out: 'Empirical investigations of institutions and political practice took the large place that traditionally had been given to the history of political thought'.[23]

Webb indeed stated that 'the purpose of the school was the application of scientific method to public and private administration'.[24] It was a view with which leading politicians agreed. The Conservative Prime Minister Arthur Balfour stated: 'It [LSE] aims at giving an education to all those who have to carry on administrative functions in this country'.[25] The Liberal politician Sir John Simon argued: 'The great function of that school must be to bring together the scientific development of certain special studies and the needs of the man of administration and of policy who must be guided and inspired thereby'.[26] Similarly, R. B. Haldane 'looked upon the school as a school where subordinate leaders were trained—men who were ready to take the general indication and work it out, and who were not afraid to take the responsibility that was put upon them.'[27] It is a great credit to the founders of the School that its place in training future leaders was acknowledged after just over a decade of the School's existence.

The Identity of the School

The early identity and profile of the School was ambiguous. In its early years, the School was intimately related to wider concerns over Britain losing ground in trade, technical expertise and scientific research. Before the School opened, *The Times* advertised the School's business courses (Commercial Geography,

---

[20] Den Otter 2007: 37–39.
[21] Ibid.: 61; Howe interview 2020.
[22] Den Otter 2007: 56.
[23] Ibid.: 62.
[24] *The Times* 1910b: 7.
[25] *The Times* 1906a: 14.
[26] *The Times* 1907b: 4.
[27] *The Times* 1911b: 15.

Commercial History, Commercial and Industrial Law, Banking and Currency) under the heading 'Higher Commercial Education'. By 1896, 'Railway Economics' had emerged as a field of study.[28]

By 1897, T. A. Organ, Chairman of an LCC Special Committee dealing with the subject, spoke on 'The Need for Systematic Commercial Education'. For such men and groups, the LSE was primarily a commercial school, competing with similar institutions in Germany, France, Russia and Austria. Organ voiced a familiar refrain: 'At present in the higher branches of commercial life the foreigner holds the field, but there was no reason why he should continue to do so provided we supplied systematic training for our native talent.'[29]

If this was a common theme in the School's early years, it was partly a reflection of the LSE struggling to establish its identity. Collaboration with the LCC and London Chamber of Commerce was largely responsible for foreign trade, commercial law, railway economics and banking courses at the School.[30] Even Lord Rosebery spoke of the School in commercial terms, a theme echoed in the press to the point of suggesting that Political Science should be jettisoned from the School's name:

> Whether or not the School of Economics—which might, perhaps, abandon, without disadvantage, the too wide and indefinite claim to be also a school of 'political science'—can fill the gap of which Lord Rosebery speaks we do not undertake to say. But the value of its work has already been practically recognised by practical men.[31]

The admixture between the School's emerging academic profile and its vocational business syllabus was often remarked on: 'The work of the school is arranged in the following groups, some of which are appropriate for University Honours in the Faculties of Arts, Laws, and Economics, and some for professional, commercial, and administrative purposes'.[32]

Alon Kadish has convincingly argued that the School was a university and a business school, and indeed the School's positive impact on commercial education was often praised.[33] As Anthony Howe suggests, vocational subjects were a 'money-spinner', generating revenue for the School and, though eventually

---

[28] *The Times*, 27 September 1895, p. 7; *The Times* 1896a: 5; *The Times* 1896b: 12.

[29] *The Times* 1897a: 10.

[30] *The Times* 1898a: 12.

[31] *The Times*, 22 March 1901, p. 9.

[32] *The Times* 1908a: 13.

[33] Dahrendorf 1995: 60; Sir Arthur Rucker, Principal of University of London, stated that approximately 900 students had studied business-related subjects; *The Times* 1902a: 10.

disappearing from the syllabus, had led to the School having a foothold, presence and visibility in financial and commercial circles and the City of London.[34]

The Founding Faculty

While the value of 'political science' was questioned, the subject, such as it was, peacefully co-existed with the vocational curriculum easily enough. As we have seen, political science at LSE was based on empirical, positivist inquiry, and aimed at making an impact on public policy. Early Calendars indicate the empiricist rather than speculative aspects of political studies, with lectures on Comparative Politics, Political Economy and Administrative History, while Constitutional History in its many forms remained a bulwark.

The historical evolution of local government and its relations with central government was a particular interest of Webb and Wallas. Indeed, the School briefly recruited the renowned statistician, political economist and folklorist of local institutions, Sir G. L. Gomme, who taught Public Administration between 1896 and 1899. His six lectures on 'The Principles of Local Government' delivered at the LSE in 1897 were an early School publication.[35] Many early lectures were published in a series of books edited by William Hewins entitled *Studies in Economics and Political Science*.[36] This empirical and historicist trend was reflected in further publications, including Frederick Galton's collection of documents relating to trade unionism, Edwin Cannan's history of local rates in England and comparative European political studies, including Bertrand Russell's Lectures on German Social Democracy.[37]

In the School's first term, 'Political Science' was one of the nine subject areas. Full-time, three-year courses were offered in Economics and Political Science, with the latter dominated, at least initially, by Graham Wallas, who conducted a 20-lecture series on 'The English constitution since 1832' with 'lectures on the growth of political theory and comparative study of foreign constitutions' also listed, a course students completed in their second year. A final, research-based course completed the third year of study.[38] Anyone could attend lectures or classes of any single course. General lectures were supposed to operate as 'feeders' for more specialised, advanced courses.[39] For someone who has been described as critical of studying comparative institutions and constitutions,

---

[34] Howe interview 2020.

[35] *The Times* 1897b: 6; *The Times*, 2 December 1897, p. 11; review in *The Times*, 7 January 1898, p. 7; *Daily Mail*, 10 December 1897.

[36] *The Times* 1897d: 6; Den Otter 2007: 62–63.

[37] Notice of publication, *The Times*, 11 March 1896, p. 12; review of Cannan, *The Times*, 13 March 1896, p. 13; *The Times*, 26 October 1898, p. 5.

[38] LSE 1895: 9–11.

[39] Kadish 1993: 237.

Wallas spent quite some time teaching these subjects. Nevertheless, these subjects did at least meet the criteria of empirical scientific methods rather than the speculative philosophy so common at Oxbridge.[40]

The curriculum of the School, Political Science included, was subject to some criticism. The economist Alfred Marshall stated that early lecture lists were determined more by who was available rather than by educational considerations. While there may have been some truth to Marshall's claims, it was inevitable that it would take time to establish a capable intellectual cadre across the School.[41] In the first prospectus, only 11 lecturers were named—nearly half remained with the School for 30 years or more, and this great longevity meant there was a remarkable degree of academic continuity at the School between 1895 and 1920.[42]

In appointing academic staff, merit, knowledge and expertise free of the cloying influence of religious orthodoxy, class, status and political affiliation were the key considerations in the Webbs' approach. Nevertheless, they had difficulty attracting those who shared their vision of political science. After advertising a one-year post for a lecturer in Political Science, Beatrice Webb was disappointed by the limitations of the candidates and their respective interests:

> Making arrangements to start the London School in its new abode at Adelphi Terrace in October ... Advertising of Political Science Lecturer—and yesterday interviewed candidates—a nondescript set of University men. All hopeless from our point of view—All imagined that Political Science consisted of a knowledge of Aristotle and 'modern'(!) writers such as De Tocqueville—wanted to put the students through a course of Utopias from More downwards. When Sidney suggested a course of lectures to be proposed on the different systems of municipal taxation, when Graham suggested a study of the rival methods of election from ad-hoc to proportional representation, the wretched candidates looked aghast and thought evidently that we were amusing ourselves at their expense. One of them wanted to construct a 'Political Man' from whose imaginary qualities all things might be deduced, another wanted to lecture on Land under the Tudors but had apparently read only the ordinary textbooks. Finally, we determined to do without our lecturer—to my mind a blessed consummation. It struck me always as a trifle difficult to teach a science which does not yet exist.[43]

Beatrice Webb's waspish and sardonic comments reflected her surprise at being confronted by the absence of political science and political scientists in Britain.

---

[40] Bevir 1997: 285.
[41] Coats 1967: 411.
[42] Hayek 1946: 5.
[43] *The Times*, 13 May 1896, p. 15; *BW Diaries*, vol. 16: 14 July 1896, 53.

Consequently, the School decided not to appoint another lecturer, and the Cambridge Fellow Lowes Dickinson appears to have been appointed to a teaching role.

The reality was that there was a relative lack of specialist teachers of politics— most of those teaching 'Political Science' had taken a first degree in Humanities, usually History, Philosophy or the Classics. Even as late as 1966, nearly 40% of the university teachers of Politics and Political Science in Britain had taken History as a first degree.[44] Perhaps inevitably, given the Oxbridge historicist tradition, none of the teaching staff between 1895 and 1920 possessed a Political Science degree.

The personnel of the early years were suitably eclectic, from the Fabianism and liberalism of Wallas and F. W. Hirst to the tariff reform conservatism of Hewins, Mackinder and Sir Percy Ashley. The broad range of political views was consistent with the Webbs' intention to source knowledge, information and expertise free from political considerations. As Friedrich Hayek observed:

> Politics entered no more than through Webb's conviction that a careful study of the facts ought to lead most sensible people, to socialism; but he took great care to select the staff from all shades of political opinion, more anxious to bring promising men under the influence of the new institution than to have it dominated by any one kind of outlook.[45]

Even friendship did not influence staff choice and tenure. The third Director of the School, William Pember Reeves, complained, when pressed to resign by Sidney Webb, that Webb 'was ruthless in the pursuit of his causes and allowed no personal considerations, either on his own behalf or of that of his friends, to stand in the way of the success of an institution or a movement he believed in'. Beatrice Webb noted this as a compliment of Webb's disinterested and meritocratic approach, when Pember Reeves had meant it as an admonishment.[46]

The previous Director, Halford Mackinder, also held different, though not entirely opposite, views to the Webbs, but the relationship remained highly professional. As Beatrice Webb wrote: 'It is an instance of the absence of a common creed—our views are not mutually antagonistic—but they never meet and would never meet if we went on working for all eternity.'[47] It was undoubtedly one of the School's strengths that it was not beholden to a self-imposed ideological straitjacket. That was largely the work of the Webbs, who were highly lauded by contemporaries for their literary and educational efforts as a 'singularly bright example of a literary partnership between husband and wife'.[48]

---

[44] Kavanagh 2007: 100.
[45] Hayek 1946: 5.
[46] *BW Diaries*, vol. 35: 29 April 1919: 32; Dahrendorf 1995: 133.
[47] *BW diaries*, vol. 26: 19 May 1908, 121.
[48] *Daily Mail*, 31 December 1897.

In the period between 1895 and 1920, there were only nine permanent lecturers in the two strands of 'Public Administration' (PA) and 'Political Science' (PS).[49] They were as follows:

- Percy Ashley (History and PA, 1899–1908);
- Goldsworthy Lowes Dickinson (PS, 1896–1920);
- H. A. Grimshaw (PA, 1917–1928);
- F. W. Hirst (PS, 1897–1900);
- Hastings B. Lees-Smith (PA, 1906–1941);
- William Piercy, first Baron Piercy (PA, 1913–1917);
- Hon W. Pember Reeves (PA, 1896–1918);
- Graham Wallas (PS, 1895–1932); and
- Sidney Webb, first Baron Passfield (PA, 1895–1927).

None possessed a formal political science training or background—Ashley, Dickinson, Hirst and Wallas were primarily historians. The importance of a classical education is plainly apparent: Ashley, Hirst, Lees-Smith and Wallas all went to Oxford, while Lowes Dickinson attended Cambridge, Pember Reeves was educated in New Zealand, and both Piercy and Grimshaw studied at the LSE for the BSc (Econ). Webb had attended Birkbeck College and King's College London before being entered for the Bar.

In 1912, Webb received the honorary title of Professor of Public Administration, though he had been an occasional lecturer since the School's formation.[50] We also find 28 occasional lecturers for the period 1895–1932, listed in the Register published in 1934, consistent with Dahrendorf's observation that the LSE possessed a 'galaxy of Occasional Lecturers'. The list includes some of the great minds of the period, including A. V. Dicey (PS), 1896–1899, Elie Halevy (PS), 1912–1913 and Beatrice Webb (PA), 1895–1901, 1903–1906 and 1915–1916. This dazzling intellectual cohort testifies to the School's increasing intellectual lustre.[51] The occasional lecturers were as follows:

- Mabel Atkinson (PA), 1901–1902;
- Ernest Barker (PS), 1912–1913;
- Sir J. A. Cockburn (PS), 1910–1911;
- C. Dalgleish (PA), 1909–1910;
- A. V. Dicey (PS), 1896–1899;
- Vicente Echeverria (PS), 1910–1911;
- Sir C. H. Firth (PS) 1896–1897;

---

[49] LSE Registrar 1934.

[50] Hayek 1946: 18; for example, three lectures on 'The Policy of Trade Unions with regards to their processes and machinery', *The Times* 1897b: 6; local government, *The Times*, 10 May 1900, p. 12; and unemployment, *The Times*, 27 January 1910, p. 11.

[51] Dahrendorf 1995: 59; LSE Registrar 1934; Hayek 1946: 11–12.

- R. C. Glen (PA), 1898–1899;
- Sir G. L. Gomme (PA), 1896–1899;
- Élie Halévy (PS), 1912–1913;
- J. H. Harley (PS), 1911–1912;
- E. J. Harper (PA), 1895–1897;
- John Kemp (PS), 1896–1598;
- G. F. McCleary (PA), 1902–1903;
- Sir Donald Maclean (PA), 1901–1902;
- J. D. Pennington (PA), 1907–1908;
- Marion Philips (PA), 1911–1912;
- E. T. Powell (PA), 1909–1911;
- Hon. Josiah Quincy (PA), 1899–1900;
- Prof. F. F. Roget (PA), 1910–1912;
- Sir Herbert Samuel (PA), 1904–1905;
- Arthur Sherwell (PA), 1899–1900;
- Sir Henry Slesser (PA), 1909–1911;
- F. H. Spencer (PA), 1902–1903;
- Sir Charles J. Stewart (PA), 1913–1914;
- Sir Frank Swettenham (PA), 1903–1914;
- Beatrice Webb (PA), 1895–1901, 1903–1906, 1915–1916; and
- C. N. Sidney Woolf (PS), 1913–1914.

Future luminaries, most notably, J. M. Keynes (MA) with a course of lectures on 'Indian Trade and Finance', also began teaching during this period.[52]

Wallas and Webb infused their passion for higher education and its public policy objectives into the School.[53] Over his long tenure, Wallas held numerous posts, possessing lectureships as political theorist, political scientist and constitutional historian. While those teaching Public Administration and Political Science had no Convener or Head, Wallas was undoubtedly *primus inter pares* of the proto 'department'. His historical expertise, interests and background were plain to see from his highly regarded publication *The Life of Francis Place, 1771–1854* (1894), which implicitly displayed the author's admiration and respect for the sturdy radicalism of the lower middle class in mid-Victorian Britain.

As Professor of Political Science, 1895 to 1923, and Professor Emeritus, 1923 to 1932, Wallas taught at the LSE for 37 years. Students regarded him as 'the permanent member of the Department of Political Science'.[54] On his appointment as Emeritus Professor, he was described as 'one of the best loved teachers in the School of Economics', which he made 'not merely a centre of research,

---

[52] *The Times* 1911c: 11.
[53] LSE 1906: 13.
[54] W. H. B. et al. 1923: 169–170.

but a centre of research that had coordination and design.[55] His most famous work, *Human Nature in Politics* (1908), outlined his unique emphasis on political psychology, though his attacks on rational political behaviour did not gain him many adherents in Britain. There was a gap in research interests and objectives between Wallas and the Webbs, pithily interpreted by Wallas, and related by Alfred Zimmern, which was considered in terms of a battle between human agency and institutions: Wallas was interested in town councillors, while Webb was interested in town councils.[56]

Alongside Webb and Wallas in the early cohort of the School was Goldsworthy Lowes Dickinson, who taught Political Science between 1896 and 1920. In 1911, he was placed on the permanent staff as a 'Lecturer in Political Science'.[57] Described as 'always accessible to pupils and students', Dickinson's 'somewhat wizened and dusky features were irradiated by a very beautiful and welcoming smile, and his voice had a sweet if husky timbre that lent, together with his eager laugh, a great charm to his talk'. Dickinson succeeded to a Fellowship at King's College, Cambridge in Neo-Platonic philosophy in 1887, before his appointment to a History lectureship in 1896. His father had been a founding member of the Working Men's College and an active Christian Socialist. Dickinson himself was actively involved in socialist circles, especially arguing for an end to 'secret diplomacy' via the Union of Democratic Control.[58]

A notable feature of the early years was the transition of those who had obtained Russell Scholarships, with £100 per annum for two years, to teaching positions. The Studentship required the recipient to deliver a short course of lectures at the end of two years, which acted for some as a platform towards an academic career. Funded by Bertrand Russell, the recipient was expected to 'devote himself to the investigation of some subject in Economics or Political Science'. The Political Science papers consisted of Ancient Constitutions, Modern Constitutions, Theory and History of the English Constitution and a general paper. F. W. Hirst, the first recipient in 1896, was, for the next three years, a lecturer on municipal and local government. He was editor of *The Economist* from 1907 to 1916, a prominent Cobden Club member and a liberal internationalist, promoting doctrines of peace, economy and free trade.[59] Percy Ashley, a graduate from Lincoln College, Oxford, obtained a Russell Scholarship in 1898, and lectured on History and Public Administration from 1899 to 1908.[60] Ashley was a younger brother of the economic historian Sir William Ashley, and father of the historian Maurice Ashley. Always primarily interested in commercial policy, he held numerous posts at the Board of Trade, acted as

---

[55] Ibid.: 170; Kavanagh 2007: 104–105.
[56] Weiner 1971: 29.
[57] Cox 2018.
[58] LSE 1906: 12; *The Times* 1908b: 11; *The Times* 1932: 12.
[59] *The Times*, 11 August 1896, p. 9; *The Times* 1953: 8; Hayek 1946: 10.
[60] LSE 1906: 11; *The Times* 1898c: 7; Hayek 1946: 10.

an advisor to Arthur Balfour, and in the 1930s served as Secretary and member of the Import Duties Advisory Committee.[61]

Other academics played a similar multi-faceted role. William Pember Reeves (1857–1932), a New Zealand journalist and politician, and New Zealand High Commissioner in London prior to his appointment with LSE, was associated with the Fabian Society from an early date. He taught Public Administration between 1896 and 1918, while simultaneously serving as Director of the School between 1908 and 1919.[62] Other members of the department included H. A. Grimshaw (PA, 1917–1928), and Hastings B. Lees-Smith (PA, 1906–1941). Lees-Smith had a long career at the LSE. Initially a Liberal, he joined the Labour Party in 1919 and led the party when Attlee joined the wartime Coalition Government in 1940.[63] Grimshaw was an LSE BSc (Econ.) graduate and recipient of the Hutchinson Research Studentship during the First World War. He argued that under-consumption was a key economic problem. At a Ruskin College Conference to discuss 'Trades Unions and Output', he suggested that 'so long as there were high incomes on one hand and next to no incomes on the other there would be produced more than enough of the luxuries and less of the necessities of life. The industrial machine produced too many ballet girls and banquets and too few boots and too little bread'.[64]

William Piercy, first Baron Piercy (PA, 1913–1917), subsequently had an illustrious career as an economist, civil servant, businessman and financier. Piercy had been a full-time undergraduate at the LSE from 1910, studying at night, and graduating with a BSc in 1914, when he was the recipient of the Mitchell Studentship to conduct research on 'The System of Local Finance in France, and Germany in their effects on Business Enterprise'.[65] He served at the Ministry of Supply and Ministry of Aircraft Production in the Second World War, was raised to the peerage on 14 November 1945, and served as a Director of the Bank of England (1946–1956) and Chairman of the Wellcome Trust (1960–1965). He retained his academic interests to the end of his life, serving as a Governor of the LSE, and a member of the Court and Senate of the University of London.[66]

Overall, the teaching of Political Science and Public Administration attracted a wide array of talented individuals. If there was a slightly left-leaning tendency, it was of a liberal left and a Labourist persuasion rather than towards Marxian socialism. While we can detect a clear concern with ethics in politics, which ranged from embracing under-consumption theories to greater transparency

---

[61] Lecturing on 'State Promotion of Foreign Commerce', *The Times* 1912a: 9; *The Times*, 14 September 1945, p. 7.
[62] *The Times* 1908c: 9; Donnelly 2016.
[63] LSE 1906: 13.
[64] *The Times*, 28 December 1916, p. 3; *The Times* 1920a: 14.
[65] *The Times* 1914a: 11.
[66] LSE 1914: 35; *The Times*, 9 July 1966, p. 10.

in foreign policy, it is fair to say that conservative positions were well-represented, especially when connected to imperial defence and tariff policy. The Webbs themselves were involved in the 'co-efficiency' movement which in a non-partisan way, was concerned with empire, social reform, and eugenics, and which brought together many people of different political persuasions.[67]

The LSE student body in the early years was different from that of Oxbridge. Wallas spoke of the LSE students as 'mainly of the type to which I had become accustomed in the University Extension movement—a few ambitious young civil servants and teachers, and a few women of leisure interested in the subject or engaged in public work'.[68] Undoubtedly, the business and vocational courses offered at the School and the evening classes provided the basis for a student body which was less classically inclined and far less likely to have been educated privately at the great public schools. Anthony Howe argues that the 'typical' LSE student of the first decades of the School's existence was 'lower middle class' in status and 'rather similar to Webb', with the School generally for the 'aspiring lower middle classes'.[69]

The School witnessed a substantial increase in numbers before 1914 and after the declining numbers during the war witnessed an upsurge after demobilisation in 1918. Over the period 1895 to 1920, a large number of students attended the LSE. By 1906, more than 5,000 students had attended since 1895. Each session witnessed a progressive increase, with, for example, 542 students in 1901–1902 rising to 1,635 (including 82 foreign students) in 1906–1907.[70]

The First Courses

The first 25 years of the School's existence witnessed a rapid expansion of what we might term the 'proto-department'. The initial focus of political studies on local, central and imperial government and the fundamental principles of political and constitutional theory were driven largely by analysis of Britain and its colonial empire. Over time, the curriculum became more refined and focused, as the School aligned itself more with the model of the *École Libre de Sciences Politiques* in Paris.

The Anglo-centric nature of the course of study had never been complete and there was always a comparative element, but it is certainly true that the Whiggish story of Britain's political development impacted and informed the curriculum. Nevertheless, comparative analysis of foreign institutions, constitutions and governments played an important part of the curriculum, interwoven with

---

[67] Radice 1984: 146.
[68] Cited in Hayek 1946: 8.
[69] Howe interview 2020.
[70] LSE 1907: 22–23.

Figure 5: Passmore Edwards Hall, 1902; Credit: LSE Library.

other emerging 'departments' of economic and political geography, economic and political history, law, public administration and public finance.[71]

In 1900, the LSE's application to join the University of London was successful. It was a crucial moment, for the School's growth and expansion was intimately tied to its place within London University. By 1902, the LSE functioned as a School of the University's newly formed 'Faculty of Economics and Political Science including commerce and industry'. The credibility of the School was enhanced, and its newfound status fended off accusations that 'LSE would be devoted to [a] utopian sort of Fabian politics'. Sidney Webb was astute in his 'academic diplomacy' in his recognition that the School could occupy an important niche within the University of London.[72]

In 1901, the BSc (Econ.) and DSc (Econ.) were established as 'the first university degrees in the country devoted mainly to the social sciences' and recognised by the University of London. The LSE was the first university to incorporate a university degree mainly devoted to the social sciences, antedating the Cambridge Economics Tripos by two years. The first Final Exams of the BSc were held in 1904, and the structure of the degree remained in place until 1923. The Final Exam consisted of three compulsory papers of Economics, History, and Public Administration and Finance, two essay papers and four

---

[71] LSE 1902: 23.
[72] Howe interview 2020.

papers on one of ten special subjects from Economic History, Statistics, to the History of Political Ideas.[73]

Several revisions were made to make courses more coherent, with Political Science acting as a nexus within several of the School's emerging fields of study, drawing on other disciplines, but in the process forming a more focused syllabus based on government and administration. By 1902, more familiar courses to modern programmes emerged, and a more streamlined syllabus was the result. International and Constitutional Law and Public Administration were compulsory classes for Political Science students around which other optional courses could be taken from other disciplines. Courses were organised under four heads—Political Science, Public Administration, Local Government and Public Finance.

For the BSc (Econ.), students of Political Science studied International and Constitutional Law, and a range of Public Administration courses, consisting of:

• Economics Descriptive and Historical;
• General Economic Theory;
• The Theory and Practice of Statistics;
• The Structure and Functions of the Modern State;
• The Government of the British Empire;
• The Historical Development of Europe;
• British Constitutional History since 1760;
• Local Self-Government in England and Abroad;
• Public Finance; and
• International and Constitutional Law.

Public Administration students were also advised to attend courses on Economic Geography, the History of British and German Commercial Policy, and the policy of different countries in relation to Railways.

Under Political Science, Dickinson managed 'Government of the British Empire' and 'The Structure and Functions of the Modern State', while under Public Administration, a range of comparative historical courses were offered, including British Constitutional History since 1760 (Wallas), Outlines of European History, 751–1321 (Ashley), Renaissance and Reformation, 1321–1648, (Ashley) and Pre-Revolutionary Europe, 1648–1789 (Ashley).[74] Local Government under Webb and Ashley consisted of comparative analysis of England, Scotland (taught by Miss Atkinson) and the history and functions of municipalities in Britain and abroad. Cannan delivered courses on public finance in Britain and abroad, including local and imperial tax systems.[75] By 1902, Beatrice Webb could write: 'Our child, born only seven years ago in two back-rooms in John Street, with a few hundreds [sic] a year, from the Hutchinson

---

[73] Hayek 1946: 13–14; Dahrendorf 1995: 57.
[74] LSE 1901: 10–11, 23–24.
[75] Ibid.: 24–25.

Trust, despised by the learned folk as a "young man's" fad, is now fully grown and ready to start in the world.'[76]

The upward trajectory of the department and School was not halted by the resignation of the first Director William Hewins in 1903 and his replacement by Halford Mackinder. Beatrice Webb recorded Hewins as a 'remarkable man' for his 'audacity, enterprise, seal and skill in presenting facts and manipulating persons', whose qualities had 'served the School well against the indifference and hostility of the London business and academic world'.[77]

By 1906, Politics and Public Administration was organised into a more coherent course, offering subjects from a range of disciplines:

- Political Ideas (Dickinson and Wallas);
- British Constitution, including local government (Wallas, Lees-Smith, Holdsworth and Webb);
- Comparative Politics (Wallas);
- English Municipalities (Webb);
- Local Government Seminar (Webb and Lees-Smith);
- Public Finance (Cannan and Foxwell);
- Economics, Theory and History (Cannan, Knowles and Mackinder);
- Demography and Statistics (Bowley);
- Accounting and Business Methods (Dicksee); and
- International Law (Oppenheim).[78]

This broad range of interdisciplinary subjects, the School argued, was vital, for:

> The student of Political Science, like the student of Economics, is the better for knowing something of the whole range of economic and polit-ical subjects. The following list of lectures has been compiled, however, for a political rather than an economic, point of view, with the object of assisting candidates for Honours in the History of Political Ideas and Public Administration to frame their courses of study.[79]

By 1908, Dickinson and Wallas shared teaching duties on 'Political Ideas', while Lees-Smith dominated 'British Constitution' courses, with his courses on local government supplemented by Webb in seminars. In related areas, Mr. Pennington taught on The Government of Manchester, with a seminar by Wallas, Holdsworth taught Law and History, Wallas taught political analysis and comparative politics. Ashley taught on the British Empire. Public finance continued under Cannan and Foxwell. Economic history was taught by

---

[76] *BW diaries*, vol. 22: 30 May 1902, 29.

[77] *BW diaries*, vol. 24: 18 November 1903, 37; also resigning his economic his-tory lectureship, *The Times*, 17 December 1903, p. 9.

[78] LSE 1906: 49–50.

[79] LSE 1906: 49.

Knowles, Cannan and Lees-Smith, while Morison taught Indian economics, and subsidiary areas of demography, accounting, geography and international law remained unchanged.[80]

Political studies was strengthened by the addition of Lees-Smith, a graduate of Queen's College, Oxford, Vice-Principal of Ruskin College, and lecturer of Political Economy at University College, Bristol.[81] He helped the department attain a more cohesive structure, with a Politics and Public Administration focus, and Lees-Smith, Dickinson and Wallas remained at the forefront of strictly 'political' courses, reducing the role of Ashley, who left in 1908. It remains true that, conceptually, empirical research and study still dominated 'political science' broadly defined at the School.

It may tell us something of the School's priorities that it was organised hierarchically, with Economics first, followed by Politics and Public Administration, History, Law, Geography, Sociology, Commerce and Industry, Accounting and Business Methods, Banking, Transport, Librarianship and, finally, a course 'for the training of Officers for the higher appointments on the Administrative Staff of the Army'. Wallas taught Public Administration as part of a wider range of political and economic courses for army officers.[82] While this hierarchy reflected a preoccupation with the study of Economics and Political Science informing better governance and policymaking, it was also indicative of the increasing academic profile of the School, which continued to advance throughout the period at the expense of the vocational courses which slowly declined.

Financial and Public Policy Developments

By 1911, the LSE was the fourth largest school among the 31 Schools of the University of London.[83] The progress and success of the School was intimately linked to external factors. Before the principle of State aid for universities was established, the LSE, as a privately founded organisation, was dependent on private donations from local bodies such as the LCC, as well as student fees.[84] Early in the School's existence, LCC funding was important in financing the appointment and payment of regular teaching staff.[85] In 1889, a State grant of £15,000 per annum was made to leading University Colleges in Britain. These

---

[80] LSE 1907: 49–50.

[81] LSE 1906: 13.

[82] LSE 1907: 68.

[83] *The Times* 1911b: 15.

[84] Dahrendorf 1995: 91; Anderson 2016.

[85] Hayek 1946: 13; *The Times*, 15 February 1896, p. 11; *The Times* 1902b: 5; *The Times* 1902c: 7.

'Annual Grants in Aid' had their origins in the University Extension Movement; by 1905, the grant had increased to £100,000.[86]

Funding was dependent (via Treasury Minute, 2 June 1897) on total local income for Arts and Science of at least £4,000 per annum or receipt of fees in the same subjects to the total of at least £1,500 per annum. Recommended grants were conditional on a minimum standard of development and teaching quality content and delivery having been achieved. A Permanent Advisory Committee of the Treasury appointed by Treasury Minute in 1906 included the LSE, for the first time, within the orbit of State aid. In late 1907, the Committee proposed a grant of £500 for the next qualifying period.[87]

While praising the School's governance and teaching quality, the amalgam of business-related and academic subjects was referred to, as LSE differs 'from other recognised Colleges in that it deals only with a limited and specialised section of higher education'. The LSE was one of four institutions whose status and functions were considered as located somewhere between universities and university colleges. Nevertheless, the Committee made a further grant of £650 in 1910, increasing to £4,500 in 1911. These grants were strictly maintenance grants to meet annual expenditure on teaching and research of a 'University character and standard'.[88] After a few shaky years, by 1911, the Director William Pember Reeves described the past year as a good one for the School largely thanks to the Treasury grant, with revenue of £13,000.[89]

Establishing the School on a solid financial foundation was essential to its progress and recognition as a university rather than a business school. A vibrant teaching of Political Science and Public Administration with an influence on public policy was vitally important to this process. We see this occurring in two areas in particular between 1895 and 1920: the connection of political science to political developments, especially imperial and military organisation, and the vibrancy of political lectures in the public space.

First, as to contemporary issues, Political Science staff played a highly significant role in public policy. Imperial sentiment reached great heights in late Victorian Britain, which was reflected in the life of the School, with military and imperial elements prominent. It was perhaps inevitable that with the first two Directors being keen imperial advocates, imperial governance and the imperial mission would feature heavily, given the wide interest, including among Fabians, in the amalgam of national efficiency, social reform and empire.[90]

These developments assumed numerous forms. For example, Lees-Smith lectured in India under UK Government auspices, with a view to establishing

---

[86] *Manchester Guardian*, 24 September 1889; Board of Education 1910: 57–76.

[87] *The Times* 1906c: 10.

[88] *The Times* 1907a: 6; University Colleges 1909; *The Times* 1910a: 18; *The Times* 1912b: 7.

[89] *The Times* 1911b: 15.

[90] Dahrendorf 1995: 43–46.

Figure 6: Sir Halford Mackinder, c.1910; Credit: LSE Library.

a Faculty of Commerce at Bombay University. That visit provided the impetus for a scheme encouraging young Indian students to visit England to study political life and institutions with the ultimate objective of assisting Viscount Morley's Indian governmental reforms. The LSE was to provide a special course for Indian students who wished to study problems of Indian administration.[91] Subsequently, a cohort of Indian students studied at the School, with a range of courses focused on India and its place within Britain's colonial empire.[92]

Similar issues of administrative efficiency affected the military, which was increasingly the focus of public policy early in the 20th century. The Liberal Government, concerned at the deficiencies of the British Army revealed by the Boer War, appointed a Consultative Committee, including Sidney Webb and Mackinder, to enquire into providing training for selected officers in military administration. As a result, officers selected by the Army Council assembled at the LSE for the first experimental commercial training courses under Mackinder. Wallas assumed a leading role, teaching a wide range of political and economic Public Administration courses for the army officers' course of study. The course continued until 1914, only to be interrupted by the outbreak of war, but resumed in 1924 and continued until 1932.[93]

---

[91] *The Times* 1908d: 4; *The Times* 1909a: 12; *The Times* 1909b: 11.

[92] Hayek 1946: 17.

[93] *The Times* 1906b: 9; *The Times*, 11 January 1907, p. 7; LSE 1907: 68; *The Times* 1913c: 6; Hayek 1946: 15; Dahrendorf 1995: 39.

The School's public lectures across the period demonstrate great vibrancy, interest and insight into public policy issues. Lectures encompassed a range of contemporary political topics from bimetallism to electoral systems and local government.[94] Before 1914, the dominant themes, with numerous variations, revolved around a broad range of imperial subjects. While Hewins was Director, imperial subjects were often conflated with commercial policy, but Mackinder was far more active in promoting the Empire, in a more rounded way, though always careful to differentiate his own activities from those of the School.[95] Numerous visitors to the School spoke on the Empire, and Wallas himself delivered a lecture on 'Our Crown Colonies and Dependencies' as part of his British Constitution lecture series.[96]

Mackinder also prepared a series of 'lantern lectures on the United Kingdom for use in the colonies', as part of a Colonial Office scheme to provide British children with a better knowledge of the colonies and vice versa.[97] Mackinder stridently asserted how the 'building up of empire was to be achieved not only by an army and navy, and through policy, but also by a united, designed, carefully-planned effort in all the schools of the Empire for a generation'.[98]

Even after Mackinder's departure as Director in 1908, imperial administration, history and politics remained an important strand of political studies. A joint programme between University College London, King's College London and LSE on imperial topics, including classes and lectures by, among others, J. H. Morgan, Foxwell and Mackinder, began in 1913.[99]

The Department and the First World War

Unsurprisingly, the war deeply affected the School, in curbing the more expansive course content which was becoming apparent in the immediate pre-war period. The staple content of Political Science and Public Administration delivered by Wallas (Political Science, local government, British Empire, Civil Service) and Lees-Smith (British Constitution, local and central government, UK financial system) was supplemented by Political Ideas modules taught by Dickinson, Morgan and Wallas.[100] Courses on economic theory and history were expanded, with contributions by, among others, William Cunningham, Lees-Smith, Cannan and Eileen Power, and for Foreign and Political

---

[94] *The Times* 1897c: 5; *The Times*, 11 October 1897, p. 3; *The Times* 1898b: 12; *The Times* 1905b: 9; *The Times* 1911a: 4.

[95] For example, delivering a lecture at the Ladies' Empire Club on 'the Essentials of British Empire', *The Times* 1905a: 6.

[96] *The Times*, 23 April 1904, p. 16.

[97] *The Times*, 22 November 1904, p. 8; *The Times* 1904b: 12.

[98] *The Times* 1904a: 14.

[99] *The Times* 1913a: 4.

[100] LSE 1915: 36–39.

History and Geography contributions by Piercy, G. P. Gooch, Mantoux and Pember Reeves.[101]

The range of courses was commensurate with the School's founding principles, which were restated: 'The founders of the School contemplated, from the first, the possession of scientific training in the methods of investigation and research, and special courses of study suitable for different groups of business men, the civil and municipal services, journalism and public work.'[102] Ominously, amid increasing international tension towards the end of 1913, and fears of civil disorder and economic and social dislocation, Graham Wallas had advanced the idea of a 'small expert committee' to provide 'invaluable organisation in time of war and might discover methods for a greater, wider, and more effective co-operation in time of peace between the Army authorities and the local government authorities'.[103] While the army course he taught was suspended for the duration of the war, the Liberal politician R. B. Haldane, a long-time friend of the Webbs and supporter and benefactor of the School, praised the LSE's role in the 'wonderful mobilization in August, 1914, and in the methodical arrangement of the transport and supply services ever since'.[104]

The First World War halted the development of the School, diminishing staff and student numbers, approximately by 50%, but after 1918, the School experienced great expansion.[105] The success of the early years was built upon, with a renewed emphasis on professionalism and efficiency allied to rigorous analysis and evaluation in academic approach, providing an effective combination in reinforcing the School's identity as a dynamic, progressive force within British higher education.

Unlike during the Second World War, the School was not evacuated, but remained in London, though many buildings were requisitioned for military use, and students and staff faced the threat of enemy bombing. During the war, wartime themes underscored political and academic commentary. Sidney Webb spoke on 8 October 1915 on 'How War is affecting Democracy', followed by a course of six lectures, beginning 20 October 1915 on 'How to prevent war', with the running theme of 'Why the prevention of War is the most important problem of Political Science for this century'. Reflecting the increasing profile of government activity during the war, Professor Hobhouse presented a course of six lectures on 'The Rights and Duties of the State'.[106] War finance and credit

---

[101] Mantoux on Modern French History and Institutions, *The Times* 1913d: 4; LSE 1914: 80–81.

[102] LSE 1914: 39.

[103] *The Times* 1913b: 12.

[104] *The Times* 1915: 5; Dahrendorf 1995: 57.

[105] Dahrendorf 1995: 129–131; Stevenson 2014.

[106] LSE 1915: 35; Pember Reeves lectured on the 'Balkans and the Near East', *The Times* 1916c: 4; *The Times* 1916a: 11.

was particularly prominent in public lectures.[107] Post-war reconstruction at home and Europe, and the prospective economic strength and prospects of Britain were being considered as early as 1916.[108]

William Beveridge: A New Era

By 1918, with the end of the war pending, attention shifted to the post-war world, with close scrutiny given to geopolitics alongside staple course material on the British Constitution, the British Empire and local government. In keeping with previous Directors, Pember Reeves delivered a lecture on 'Consolidation of the Empire' nine months before the war ended. One year after the war ended, a previous Director, Mackinder, delivered a lecture series on 'The British Empire under the New Conditions of the World'.[109] The inaugural lecture of 1918–1919, 'Science and Politics' by Wallas, was a progressive acknowledgment of the great changes expected in the post-war world.

Beatrice Webb was appointed to the Reconstruction Committee under Lloyd George's government in 1917, a task she relished, and Sidney Webb's continuing influence was apparent as the war entered its final year, as the main author of Labour's 1918 manifesto 'Labour and the New Social Order', a programme for post-war reconstruction, which began with the striking phrase 'We need to beware of patchwork' and which argued for a 'deliberately thought-out systematic and comprehensive plan for the immediate social rebuilding which any Ministry, whether or not it desires to grapple with the problem, will be driven to undertake'.[110] The famous 'Clause IV' was drafted as part of the Labour manifesto, providing the intellectual rationale for widespread public ownership which was to become influential in the following years.

Within the School, the keynote in Political Science and Public Administration was continuity. Lees-Smith and Wallas still dominated Political Science and constitutional issues, and there was the same blend of local and national government which had characterised political studies since 1895. The impact of the war was predictable, with an emphasis on military and commercial geopolitical rivalry, most notably in 20 lectures by Lees-Smith on 'Political and

---

[107] Hartley Withers on credit and finance, *The Times* 1914b: 11; Foxwell on 'Some problems of war finance', *The Times* 1916d: 5; Withers and Mackinnon Wood on 'Problems of economic progress' and 'Enemy systems of food control', *The Times* 1918b: 9.

[108] Sir George Paish on 'The economic strength of Great Britain', *The Times* 1916e: 3; 'Geographical conditions of the reconstruction of Europe' by Mackinder, *The Times* 1916b: 11; Gooch on 'Problems of the settlement: Poland, Bohemia, Alsace-Lorraine', *The Times* 1917: 11.

[109] *The Times* 1918a: 9; *The Times* 1919a: 15.

[110] *The Times* 1918c: 3.

Figure 7: Celebrations following the laying of the foundation stone in Houghton Street, 28th May 1920. After the ceremony, LSE students in high spirits carried a statue of Sir Walter Raleigh through London proclaiming that he was to be enrolled as a new student; Credit: LSE Library.

social problems arising from the war' and eight lectures respectively on 'Tariffs and Tariff Administration' and 'The Budgets of the Great Powers' by renowned economist Theodore Gregory.[111]

The resignation of Pember Reeves as Director in May 1919 led to the appointment of William Beveridge, whose brilliant record of scholarship and accomplished background in journalism and the Civil Service augured well for the School.[112] Fittingly, Beveridge delivered the keynote public lecture for 1919–1920 on 'The Public Service in War and Peace'.[113] Beveridge's appointment, combined with the arrival of Harold Laski in 1920, were harbingers of significant changes of personnel and syllabus content in the 1920s which was undoubtedly healthy from an academic viewpoint.[114] Symbolic of new beginnings, George V laid the foundation stone of the main building in 1920, on a site presented by the LCC. The extension was intended to mainly accommodate the new degree of Bachelor of Commerce (BCom).[115] A set of newly minted coins and a copy of

---

[111]   LSE 1918: 35–39; Bigg 2018.
[112]   *The Times* 1919c: 6; *The Times* 1919d: 13.
[113]   *The Times* 1919b: 15.
[114]   Hayek 1946: 19; Dahrendorf 1995: 141–146.
[115]   Dahrendorf 1995: 142; *Daily Mail*, 30 March 1920.

Professor Cannan's book, *Wealth: A Brief Explanation of the Causes of Economic Wealth* (1914), were placed beneath the foundation stone.[116]

After two years as Director, Beatrice Webb was pleased with Beveridge and his approach, but reflecting on the School's history, praised her husband and his dynamism and humility, for 'beyond a few of the "old gang" no one recognises that the School is his creation and he does not wish anyone to do so'.[117] Webb's vision, hard work and integrity mean we should accord him a primary role in the evolution of the philosophy of the School and its respective departments.

As noted in the introduction, while the First World War had a significant effect on the School's progression towards maturity, the Spanish Influenza pandemic had no perceptible impact. Neither the School's own Calendars nor indeed Dahrendorf's extensive *History of the LSE* make any mention of the fact that from June 1918 to April 1919 London itself (with a population of approximately 4.5 million) suffered over 16,000 registered deaths from that pandemic.[118]

Conclusion

The political, educational, and commercial imperatives driving the School forward were all concerned with applying scientific techniques as a means of improving society, inculcating better decision-making, and advancing technical and political expertise. In many ways, the School has not moved from that position. Tony Travers is not alone in feeling a link to the original ethos of the School 'all the way back through George Jones and the Greater London Group to [William] Robson and backward from that to the Webbs'.[119]

The embryonic condition of political studies and 'political science' was in many ways a reflection of the dominance of grand narratives in political and constitutional history in Britain. It would take more than a scientific approach to research to change the contours of political science, but at least a start had been made in shifting the discipline, such as it was, from an over-emphasis on political philosophy. On a more granular basis, the School had recruited some impressive staff members and lecturers, and had shown it was serious in promoting academic study, and in the best traditions of disinterestedness, was devoted to procuring experts from different backgrounds and with different interests and political views.

As early as 1910, the LSE possessed global brand recognition. The first woman to win a scholarship endorsed by the Federation of Women's Clubs of America, Juliet Points, chose the LSE over Oxbridge 'because sociology and economics

---

[116] *The Times* 1920b: 11.

[117] *BW diaries*, vol. 36: Christmas Eve 1921, 76.

[118] Smallman-Raynor et al. 2002.

[119] Travers telephone interview 2020.

cannot be better studied than at the London School of Economics, which is famous throughout the world'.[120]

Although political science did not yet enjoy similar renown, a start had been made, and a distinctive empirical approach had emerged representing a valuable addition to the study of government and politics in British higher education. However, a greater degree of professionalism, the advance of political science as a discipline and a more formal department were, as yet, in the future.

References

Abse, J (ed.) 1977 *My LSE.* London: Robson Books.

Anderson, R 2016 University fees in historical perspective. 8 February. Available at http://www.historyandpolicy.org/policy-papers/papers/university-fees-in-historical-perspective.

Bevir, M 1997 Graham Wallas today. *Political Quarterly,* 68(3) (July–September): 284–292.

Bigg, R 2018 Theodore Gregory and early economics at LSE, 11 July. Available at https://blogs.lse.ac.uk/lsehistory/2018/07/11/theodore-gregory-at-lse/.

Board of Education 1910 Report for those Universities and University Colleges in Great Britain which participated in the Parliamentary Grant for University Colleges in the year 1908–9 [Cd. 5246], *Edinburgh Review,* 213: 435.

Coats, A W 1967 Alfred Marshall and the early development of the London School of Economics: Some unpublished letters. *Economica,* 34(136): 408–417.

Cox, M 2018 Goldsworthy Lowes Dickinson and the origins of international relations, 12 December. Available at https://blogs.lse.ac.uk/lsehistory/2018/12/12/goldsworthy-lowes-dickinson-lse-and-the-origins-of-international-relations/.

Dahrendorf, R 1995 *A history of the London School of Economics and Political Science, 1895–1995.* Oxford: Oxford University Press.

Daily Mail 1910 New scholarship scheme, 22 October.

Den Otter, S M 2007 The origins of a historical science in late Victorian and Edwardian Britain. In: Adcock, R, Bevir, N and Stimson, S C (eds.), *Modern political science: Anglo-American exchanges since 1880.* Oxford: Princeton University Press. pp. 37–65.

Donnelly, S 2015c LSE's first prospectus, 7 October. Available at https://blogs.lse.ac.uk/lsehistory/2015/10/07/lses-first-prospectus/.

Donnelly, S 2016 LSE directors, 12 September. Available at https://blogs.lse.ac.uk/lsehistory/2016/09/12/lse-directors/.

---

[120] *Daily Mail* 1910: 3.

Forster, E M 1934 *Goldsworthy Lowes Dickinson*. London: Edward Arnold.

Hayek, F A 1946 The London School of Economics, 1895–1945. *Economica*, 13(49): 1–31.

Kadish, A 1993 The City, the Fabians and the foundation of the London School of Economics. In: Kadish, A and Tribe, K (eds.), *The market for political economy: The advent of economics in British university culture, 1850–1905*. New York: Routledge. pp. 227–250.

Kavanagh, D 2007 The emergence of an embryonic discipline; British politics without political scientists. In Adcock, R, Bevir, M and Stimson, S C (eds.), *Modern political science: Anglo-American exchanges since 1880*. Oxford: Princeton University Press. pp. 97–117.

Lowes Dickinson, G 1926 *The international anarchy, 1904–1914*. New York: The Century Company.

LSE 1895 *The London School of Economics and Political Science, University of London, Calendar, 1895*. London: London School of Economics and Political Science.

LSE 1901 *The London School of Economics and Political Science, University of London, sessional programme, 1901–02*. London: London School of Economics and Political Science.

LSE 1902 *The London School of Economics and Political Science, University of London, sessional programme, 1902–03*. London: London School of Economics and Political Science.

LSE 1906 *The London School of Economics and Political Science, University of London, Calendar for twelfth session, 1906–07*. London: London School of Economics and Political Science.

LSE 1907 *The London School of Economics and Political Science, University of London, Calendar for thirteenth session, 1907–08*. London: London School of Economics and Political Science.

LSE 1914 *The London School of Economics and Political Science, University of London, Calendar for twentieth session, 1914–15*. London: London School of Economics and Political Science.

LSE 1915 *The London School of Economics and Political Science, University of London, Calendar for twenty-first Session, 1915–16*. London: London School of Economics and Political Science.

LSE 1918 *The London School of Economics and Political Science, University of London, Calendar for twenty-fourth session, 1918–19*. London: London School of Economics and Political Science.

LSE Registrar (ed.) 1934 *The London School of Economics and Political Science (University of London) Register, 1895–1932*. London: London School of Economics and Political Science. With an introduction by the Director (March).

Martin, D E 2004 Goldsworthy Lowes Dickinson (1862–1932), *Oxford Dictionary of National Biography*, 23 September. DOI: https://doi.org/10.1093/ref:odnb/32815.

Qualter, T H 1980 *Graham Wallas and the great society*. London and Basingstoke: Palgrave Macmillan.

Radice, L 1984 *Sidney and Beatrice Webb: Fabian socialists*. London and Basingstoke: Macmillan.

Smallman-Raynor, M, Johnson, N and **Cliff, A D** 2002 The spatial anatomy of an epidemic: Influenza in London and the county boroughs of England and Wales, 1918–1919. *Transactions of the Institute of British Geographers,* 27(4): 452–470.

Stevenson, D 2014 LSE and the First World War, 1 August. Available at https://blogs.lse.ac.uk/lsehistory/2014/08/01/lse-and-the-first-world-war/.

The Times 1896a 'Commercial Education', 8 October.

The Times 1896b 'Railway Economics', 6 November.

The Times 1897a 'Commercial Education', 15 October.

The Times 1897b 'Court Circular', 8 November.

The Times 1897c 'Professor Edgeworth on Bimetallism', *The Times*, 7 October.

The Times 1897d 'The London School of Economics and Political Science', 18 January.

The Times 1898a 'Commercial Education', 14 January.

The Times 1898b 'Local Government', 19 November.

The Times 1898c 'Research Studentships', 27 July.

The Times 1902a 'The London School of Economics', 11 October.

The Times 1902b 'University Intelligence', 23 January.

The Times 1902c 'University Intelligence', *The Times*, 20 June.

The Times 1904a 'Mr. Broderick on the Empire and Education', 19 December.

The Times 1904b 'The Empire and the Schools', 8 December.

The Times 1905a 'Court Circular', 26 January.

The Times 1905b 'Municipalities in England: their constitution and functions', 'Court Circular', 31 October.

The Times 1906a 'London School of Economics', 26 February.

The Times 1906b 'The Administrative Staff of the Army', 19 November.

The Times 1906c 'University Intelligence', 1 September.

The Times 1907a 'Grants to University Colleges', 9 August.

The Times 1907b 'London School of Economics: speech by Mr. Haldane', 11 February.

The Times 1908a London School of Economics, 15 September.

The Times 1908b Obituary, Mr. Lowes Dickinson, 21 December.

The Times 1908c New director of the School of Economics, 23 July.

The Times 1908d The Indian National Congress, 28 December.

The Times 1909a LSE and Indian students, 22 April.

The Times 1909b University intelligence, 23 October.

The Times 1910a Grants to university colleges, 23 April.

The Times 1910b 'London School of Economics', 7 February.

The Times 1911a Prospective arrangements, 18 February.

The Times 1911b The London School of Economics, 27 February.

The Times 1911c To-day's arrangements, 23 January.

The Times 1912a Arrangements for to-day, 8 October.

The Times 1912b Grants to universities and colleges, 12 April.

The Times 1913a Lectures on imperial subjects, 20 September.

The Times 1913b Local authorities in war time, 27 November.

The Times 1913c Naval and military intelligence, 19 June.

The Times 1913d University intelligence, 23 January.

The Times 1914a News in brief, 21 March.

The Times 1914b War and credit, 12 November.

The Times 1915 Direction of the army, 4 November.

The Times 1916a Court circular, 21 February.

The Times 1916b Court circular, 11 October.

The Times 1916c Law notices, 5 Feb, 5 February.

The Times 1916d Some problems of war finance, 29 January.

The Times 1916e The economic strength of Great Britain, 5 February.

The Times 1917 Court circular, 31 January.

The Times 1918a Arrangements for to-day, 14 February.

The Times 1918b Court circular, 6 February.

The Times 1918c Democratic control of society, 3 January.

The Times 1919a Court circular, 8 November.

The Times 1919b London School of Economics, 22 September.

The Times 1919c New professors at London university, *The Times*, 29 May.

The Times 1919d Sir William Beveridge's new post, *The Times*, 22 August.

The Times 1920a Labour's interest in output, 19 January.

The Times 1920b The King and London University: ceremony at School of Economics, 29 May.

The Times 1932 Obituary, G. Lowes Dickinson, 4 August.

The Times 1947 Obituary of Webb, 14 October.

The Times 1953 The Liberal tradition in economics, 23 February.

University Colleges (Great Britain) (Grants in Aid) 1909 Copy of Report of Advisory Committee, dated 24 July 1908, with Treasury Minute on the Committee's Report, dated 3 June 1909, House of Commons papers, *Parliamentary papers* 69 (1909), [182], LXIX.1.

Webb, B Beatrice Webb's typescript diary, vol. 16, 16 July 1895–[7 March] 1898, LSE Digital Library.

Webb, B Beatrice Webb's typescript diary, vol. 22, December 1901–5 June 1902, LSE Digital Library.

Webb, B Beatrice Webb's typescript diary, vol. 24, 15 June 1903–22 December 1904, LSE Digital Library.

Webb, B Beatrice Webb's typescript diary, vol. 26, 4 August 1906–15 November 1908, LSE Digital Library.

Webb, B Beatrice Webb's typescript diary, vol. 35, 13 October 1918– 4 September 1920, LSE Digital Library.

Webb, B Beatrice Webb's typescript diary, vol. 36, 17 September 1920–10 February 1923, LSE Digital Library.

Webb, S 1889 Socialism in England. *Publications of the American Economic Association*, 4(2): 7–73.

Weiner, M J 1971 *Between Two Worlds: The Political Thought of Graham Wallas* (Oxford: Clarendon Press)

W H B, H D and **H J L** 1923 Graham Wallas. *Economica*, 9 (November): 169–170.

Interviews

Howe, Anthony, telephone interview by Hilke Gudel, 11 May 2020.

Travers, Tony, telephone interview by Hilke Gudel, 25 March 2020.

CHAPTER 2

The Orator and the Conversationalist

From Laski to Oakeshott, 1921–1965

Daniel Skeffington

Introduction

The period that was to follow would have its tone set by the arrival of two titans of political thought: Harold Laski and Michael Oakeshott. Laski and Oakeshott's careers spanned most of the 20th century, from the former's appointment in 1920 to the latter's death in 1990. The two political theorists never crossed paths at the School, with Oakeshott moving from Oxford to take up the chair in Political Science following Laski's death in March of 1950. Both were the informal 'Conveners' of the Government department, in a time when there were no heads—or even departments—to speak of in the School, and each left their distinctive mark on the fabric of the institution.

Part of the reason the department's image was so dominated by these larger-than-life characters during the early and middle parts of the century was the interdisciplinary structure of the School. The LSE, like many institutions, had yet to develop distinct departments as such among its faculties, and most buildings involved the sharing of offices with members of different disciplines. In one sense, this reinforced the emphasis of the School's focus on the social sciences as a whole, bringing together all disciplines under one roof. Although the seeds of what would become the Department of Government had been

How to cite this book chapter:
Skeffington, D. 2021. The Orator and the Conversationalist: From Laski to Oakeshott, 1921–1965. In: Schonhardt-Bailey, C. and Bannerman, G. (eds.) *Political Science at the LSE: A History of the Department of Government, from the Webbs to COVID.* Pp. 53–85. London: Ubiquity Press. DOI: https: //doi.org/10.5334/bcn.c. License: CC-BY-NC

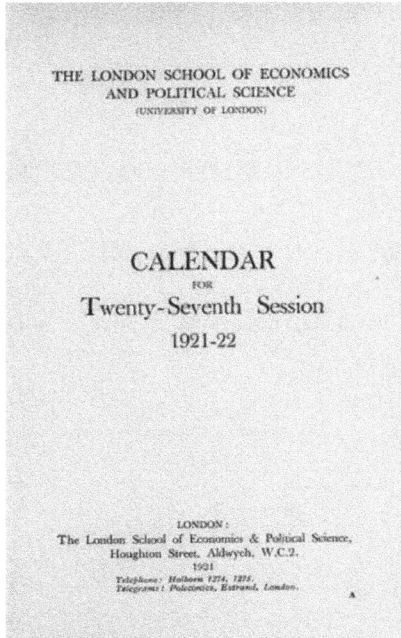

THE LONDON SCHOOL OF ECONOMICS
AND POLITICAL SCIENCE
(UNIVERSITY OF LONDON)

CALENDAR
FOR
Twenty-Seventh Session
1921-22

LONDON :
The London School of Economics & Political Science,
Houghton Street, Aldwych, W.C.2.
1921
Telephone: Holborn 1214, 1215.
Telegrams: Polecomics, Estrand, London.

A

Figure 8: First page of the Calendar for the Twenty-Seventh Session, LSE
Calendar, 1921–1922; Credit: LSE Library.

planted, expressed through the course division into matters of politics, public
and colonial administration since joining the University of London in 1900,
the reality on the ground was this was a somewhat imprecise and even ram-
shackle undertaking, collaborating between different, ill-defined groupings of
scholars whose interests happened to align. It was in this collective of thinkers
and teachers that these two scholars made their names, setting the course of the
Government Department for two generations of students to come.

Harold Laski: The 'Red Professor'

The early 1920s bore witness to the arrival of one of the Department's leading
lights. Harold Joseph Laski joined the School in the Michaelmas term of 1920,
during the 'second foundation' of the School under William Beveridge.[1] He
took Graham Wallas's Chair in Political Science in 1926, where his passionate
style of teaching would set the tone of the department during the interwar
period, a tone that dominated to the end of the Attlee Government on his death
in 1950. A brazen, youthful, socialist academic with a grasp of the broad brush

---

[1] Dahrendorf 1995: 135.

of political activity, his bombastic lecturing style and constant forays into political life soon became a hallmark of the LSE's approach to government.

As we saw in Chapter 1, despite sharing half the name of the School itself, Political Science was slow to achieve repute as a subject of study at the LSE. Indeed, when Laski took over Wallas's Chair in 1926, it was one of only two other such positions in Political Science in the United Kingdom, with one being held at Oxford, and another having just been created at Cambridge.[2] The former Director of the School, Ralf Dahrendorf, has gone as far as to describe political science at the LSE as a 'one-man band' well into the late 1920s.[3] However, this band was to be championed by the most 'widely known and most loved professor' at the School, indeed in British political life during his time. It is no surprise that 70 years after his death, many still credit him with the founding of the Government Department at the LSE, even if its formal creation was not to be until after he passed away, at the young age of 56.

Upon his arrival, Harold Laski immediately took over many of the courses in political philosophy and public administration. A long-standing member of the Fabian Society and one of the founders of the Left Book Club, Laski was a convinced socialist, leaving a mark on the department in a period when the LSE's connection with socialist societies was probably at its height. Although those reflecting on his tenure at the School have come to see him as a radical, Laski held a tempered view on what it meant to be a socialist, and a closer examination of his life and style as a professor of politics reveals this more nuanced character in full.

Laski's academic work on politics was as varied as it was influential. He was a great proponent of pluralism throughout society, promoting local and voluntarist elements of a democratic political system. Works written between 1919 and 1921 began advancing this line of thought, attacking the notion of an all-powerful sovereign power against other highly centralised notions of the state, such as the German jurist Carl Schmitt's study of *Dictatorship* and subsequent proto-fascist treatises.[4] These would form the beginnings of his academic and political struggles against totalitarian ideologies until the end of the Second World War.

His magnum opus, *The Grammar of Politics*, was first published in 1925, and formed a comprehensive examination of the history of democratic institutions. In so doing, *The Grammar* advanced arguments that would distance him from his successor, with Laski insisting there must always be a link between the practical and the theoretical in politics. During the 1930s, he became a convert of Marxism—in no small part as a reaction against the rising threat of fascism—and alongside the Webbs was convinced of its ability to produce a more

---

[2] Krammick & Sheerman 1993: 245.

[3] Dahrendorf 1995: 226.

[4] Laski 1919; Laski 1921; Schmitt 2014.

efficient, productive society. Later works from thereon in focused on the reform of capitalist economics in Britain along such lines.

Yet, the main focus of his work was always to be found in his lecturing, rather than in his written work. While his *Reflections on the Constitution*, given as three lectures one month before his death and published posthumously in 1951, remain an important text for understanding British constitutional thought, they also show this oratorical side most keenly, 'stamped with his personality', which was ever a force at the forefront of the School.[5] Jacqueline Wheldon, LSE secretarial staff (1946) and U/G and Research Student (1948–1954), recalls that his lectures at the Old Theatre were always crowded, and that he was

> magnificent at creating parables out of contemporary politics and those of the recent past. Had they been the only thing he had to offer he could not have been so influential a teacher. The most important thing about him was that he was a generous man of lively temper who desired, even when it was impossible to perform what he desired, 'to confirm the low-liest in the possibility of what they might become' as much as he relished the company of the great and powerful.[6]

He was fondly remembered by many students for just this, and while he pos-sessed a tortuous writing style remarked on by George Orwell himself,[7] his freestyle lecturing was considered an intellectually brilliant tour de force.

Laski's oratorical presence also extended beyond academia, and into politi-cal life itself. Laski held the Labour Party Chairmanship from 1945 to 1946, regularly speaking at events that furthered socialist causes, in his memorably bombastic style. Laski's guiding objective during his studies was benevolently described by the former Labour MP and socialist Ian Mikardo: 'His mission in life was to translate the religion of the universal brotherhood of man into the language of political economy.'[8]

So great was his reputation as a lecturer that the young John F. Kennedy travelled to the School in 1935 to take his classes on the General Course. His brother, Joe, had studied under the young H. R. G. Greaves and K. B. Smellie— two central figures in the department's history—in 1933, and it was his father Joe Kennedy's intention that the future president would follow suit. A per-sonal friend of the family, Laski had been recommended by Felix Frankfurter, who remarked he was 'the greatest teacher in the world'.[9] Unfortunately,

---

[5] Laski 2015: prefatory note.

[6] Abse 1977: 136.

[7] Orwell 2013.

[8] Neil Clark, "Harold Laski – the man who influenced Ralph Miliband," New Statesman (3 January 2013), https://www.newstatesman.com/politics/uk -politics/2013/01/harold-laski-man-who-influenced-ralph-miliband.

[9] Donnelly 2015.

J. F. Kennedy fell unexpectedly ill before he could commence his studies, and left London without attending a single course.

His gifts as a teacher notwithstanding, Laski also gathered his fair share of criticism from both sides of the political spectrum. He embodied a certain academic activism that was lost on the Department's later star intellectuals; one unafraid to shy away from controversy or criticism. His vocal and combative demeanour earned him a measure of disdain, particularly among fellow socialists; he was most famous for being on the receiving end of a barb from Attlee that 'I can assure you there is widespread resentment in the Party at your activities and a period of silence on your part would be welcome' after Laski had appeared to be speak on behalf of the Labour Government and its foreign policy.[10] Indeed, the tension between academic freedom and political expediency was sometimes a problem during the Laski era. After accusations that Laski travelled to Moscow to speak to the 'Communist Academy', Clement Attlee refuted these allegations, stating that Laski spoke to the Institute of Socialist Law, and in doing so, robustly defended the principle of parliamentary sovereignty. Replying to the accusation that Laski was a communist and alien, and had been permitted by the LSE to 'spread his poisonous propaganda', Sir Stafford Cripps stated: 'Is the Hon. Member aware that the Charter of the London School of Economics expressly provides for complete freedom for professors and lecturers to express their political opinions outside the school, and will he resist the obvious tendency to try to curtail this freedom.'[11]

Despite these high-profile run-ins with peers and critics for his radicalism, he retained a fairly incremental and progressive approach to actual social reform, reflecting the wishes of the founders of the School in this respect. Beatrice and Sidney Webb, alongside Graham Wallas and George Bernard Shaw, had set out a vision for the School as one of moderate change, devoted to social reform through established, rather than disruptive, methods. His was a democratic socialism based on the gradual change of society through parliamentary democracy, and although he supported the 'Hands off Russia' movement, which saw dockers refuse to load ships destined to help Poland fight against the Soviet Union, he opposed the advocates of 'direct action' that dominated the Left at the time. He believed in mediation and progress through parliamentary means over direct action, leading to a reputation among some peers as a snob of the workers' movement. Yet, Laski was committed, as many of his colleagues were, to promoting the School as an alternative to the traditional ancient universities, dedicated to meaningful and practical education for a new, more equitable society. He consistently declined to stand as Labour MP because of his love of academic life and his belief in the importance of ideas.[12] It seems his apparently snobbish attitudes separated him from the wider Labour movement at times, including one anecdote he wrote about in a letter

---

[10] Newman 1993: 268.
[11] Hansard, HC Deb. 11 July 1934, Vol. 292, cc. 306–308.
[12] Newman 1993: 76.

to Oliver Wendell Holmes in which he said he was shocked to see a Labour MP finish off another's half-drunk beer.[13]

Laski's political direction and professional trajectory were heavily shaped by his friendships and personal correspondences. He ran in the upper echelons of international society, reflected through his contacts in the world of politics and law. He maintained relationships from his period in the United States which went on to shape changes in his ideas, giving him a sort of American streak to his political thinking. Samuel Baron in the *Clare Market Review* commented that 'many Americans found it difficult to believe that he was not American'. One figure who played a large role in the evolution of Laski's thinking was his long-standing friend, the US Supreme Court Justice and Harvard law professor Oliver Wendell Holmes, with whom he developed a close personal correspondence following his studies at McGill University. Indeed, Laski came to consider Holmes as his 'American father', and the relationship of the two strengthened the School's early transatlantic ties.[14] The regular correspondence between the two gives an interesting summary on Laski's ideas on several topics, including religion and policy. Laski writes to Holmes that he was opposed to the favouring of any one religion under law and, while he believed that religion had an inherent beauty, this was its only appeal. He also opposed attempts to reconcile religion and science, which he saw as irreconcilable. In terms of policy, he writes that the 'only adequate test for good [is] social utility and this meant response to demand of persons ... if there was a God it was an everyday God, discoverable in everyday good'.[15] In his letters with Holmes, some of the theoretical grounding of Laski's scepticism also comes through. Laski also maintained an international presence thanks to the influence of his academic works. This is particularly the case with Laski's connection to India. In 1930, Laski became the President of the 'India League', a British-based organisation which campaigned for the 'full independence and self-government' of India. Seven years after India claimed its independence, the Indian Government founded the Harold Laski Institute of Political Science in the city of Ahmedabad, at the time the capital of the province of Gujarat, in recognition of his contributions to the nation.[16] One Indian politician is even said to have claimed 'in every meeting of the Indian Cabinet there is a chair reserved for the ghost of Professor Harold Laski'.[17]

These international links were primarily formed during a crucial change of emphasis in Laski's political outlook, following his return to the United Kingdom in 1919, the same year William Beveridge took over as Director of the School. Coming back from the United States, Laski began to share more

---

[13] Ibid.: 73.
[14] Dahrendorf 1995: 225.
[15] de Wolfe Howe 1953: 909.
[16] LSE Library n.d.
[17] Shearhard 2014: 157.

Figure 9: Professor Harold Laski. Credit. Alamy.

political ideas with the Liberal Party despite still being a Labour Party supporter. Around this time, he began his correspondence with Liberal Cabinet Minister Lord Haldane, who played a role in Laski's appointment to the LSE. Haldane influenced Laski's interest in adult education as a crucial part of the worker's engagement in social change. Around this time, Laski also took up a position at Haldane's Institute of Adult Education. Laski became very interested, alongside Haldane, in forming an alliance between the Liberal and Labour Parties. While he shared the convictions of the Labour Party, he seemed to find it easier to relate to the Liberal Party and, more specifically, its members. He told Arthur Gleason that he found his comfort 'largely in the people outside the Labour movement altogether'.[18]

Alongside his strong personal relationships and correspondences, Laski also had much support and appreciation among his students. In a memorial edition of the *Clare Market Review* marking his death, students talked of his 'special talent [to] communicate with students on a common ground of understanding', but also mentioned his 'innocent and forgivable vanity'. There was a running joke about his radicalism among the students, who performed imitations of Laski along the lines of 'and so I said to Stalin ...'.

---

[18] Newman 1993: 74.

Not all were so in awe of the department's famous professor, however. Laski was the direct inspiration for Ayn Rand's character Elsworth Toohey in *The Fountainhead*, embodying

> the soul of Ellsworth Toohey in the flesh … his mannerisms, the pseudo-intellectual snideness, the whole manner of speaking on important subjects with inappropriate sarcasm as his only weapon, acting as if he were a charming scholar in a drawing room, but you could sense the bared teeth behind the smile, you could feel something evil.[19]

Interestingly, she writes that Toohey is 'not a member of the Communist Party, because that Party is still considered working class', alluding to his slight snobbish removal from the roots of the socialist movement.[20] He was also not regarded as a particularly strong writer, with George Orwell using his work as an example of bad writing in his essay on *Politics and the English Language*. Orwell cited a 53-word sentence, including five negatives, which appeared in Laski's *Essay in Freedom of Expression*, which Orwell thought illustrated 'various of the mental vices' present in writing.[21] However, their attacks on the 'red professor', as he humorously became known, and were few and far between, and were water off the back of a man whose lecturing far eclipsed the impact of his written work.

The Department under Laski: A 'One-Man Band'?

During Laski's tenure as informal leader of the political scientists at the School, the proto department flourished. As had been the case in the early years under Wallas, it is difficult to describe this in any real sense as analogous to the modern idea of a 'Government' Department. This sense was to prevail well into the 1950s, when the late Professor of Middle Eastern politics, Elie Kedourie, arrived as an undergraduate. As Alan Beattie put it, for the first half of the School's life, politics was far more a subject, rather than a discipline, as had been the founders' intention.[22] That is, the bridge between (1) politics, policy and political action, and (2) the conceptual underpinnings of politics as a discipline was, as yet, underdeveloped.

Nevertheless, under Laski, the cohort of scholars at the School focusing on political science continued to grow, creating the foundations of the modern discipline through their interests. These courses were grouped under the loose name of Politics and Public Administration in the School's Calendar, and could

---

[19] Rand & Peikoff 1999: 85.
[20] Ibid.: 84.
[21] Orwell 2013: 3.
[22] Beattie 1998: 110.

be taken on a range of BA courses in, for example, History or Sociology, to graduate within the framework of 'Honours in the History of Political Ideas or Public Administration', which would 'frame their courses of study'.[23]

This early model followed the School's integrated approach to the social sciences, believing there to be a central 'core' of subjects one must study, but which one could approach from a variety of angles. As the years progressed, students would not only work towards their specialisation in the political sciences as a subdomain of the social sciences, but as an autonomous field-in-itself. In the 1920s, the subject was acquiring its academic credibility among British institutions, much as economics had had to do in the previous century, and which sociology was not to attain until well after the conclusion of the Second World War. Therefore, even if the term 'proto department' might be somewhat of a stretch during Laski's early years, it certainly captures the drive that spurred on research and teaching at the time, that is as a collective of scholars feeling its way around unfamiliar but fallow ground.

These were very much the School's adolescent years, then, with the department developing its reputation as a centre for colonial administration and public policy, as well as political thought. Courses were run on 'The Government of British India' by Professor John Coatman, 'British Colonial Policy' by Professor Kingsley Smellie and the 'French Colonial Office' by the distinguished historian Professor Paul Vaucher.[24] There was much overlap in this period with the School's academic lawyers, who contributed to the intersection of administrative and constitutional law with public administration, such as Ivor Jennings's 1935 class on 'Colonial Constitutional Law'.[25] More contentious classes, such as 'The Genetical Theory of Inbreeding', occasionally ran alongside these, but on the whole the focus was on comparative public administration of the colonies.[26] Political thought also began to take centre stage, with Laski personally running courses on 'Political Ideas of the Ancient World', 'European Political Ideas', 'Medieval Political Ideas' and 'Political Ideas since 1689'.[27] Others joined him in lecturing on English, American and French political ideas, from time to time, as the years went on.

One of the most important figures among this cohort was Kingsley Bryce (K. B.) Smellie, who joined the School in 1921 as its first Professor in Political Science. Smellie was to prove influential in Laski's departmental reinvigoration. He would lecture frequently on public administration and was later given a personal named Chair in 1949 for his services to the field, which he held until his retirement in 1965. Smellie also developed political thought at the School, running classes on American political ideas both pre- and post-Civil War

---

[23] LSE 1935: 1935–36.
[24] Eliot 2016.
[25] LSE 1935: 208.
[26] Ibid.
[27] Ibid.: 207–212.

Figure 10: Kingsley B. Smellie (Left) and Graham Wallas (Right), 1925; Credit: LSE Photo Archives.

alongside Laski, as well as 'English Political Thought in the Nineteenth Century'. By the middle of Laski's term heading the political scientists at the LSE, the BSc (Econ.) degree for which the School became famous was offering these sorts of courses as a pathway to obtain the specialisation in Government, and students looking to graduate with a degree from the Government department would take special subjects like Smellie's 'English Constitution' to account for this on their transcript. Other students, such as those enrolled on the BA (Hons) in Sociology, could also take these courses to count towards their own specialisation. All this points towards the nascent image of the Government department as a sort of 'style' of approach to the greater study of the economics and political sciences at the School, which had by now cemented its reputation as the Faculty of Economics within the larger University of London.

Another major addition was the LSE graduate and Fabian socialist Herman Finer, who joined the School in 1920 to lecture on public administration, until departing in 1942 for the University of Chicago.[28] Finer would serve as a major assistant to Laski on constitutional courses, particularly 'The British Constitution', 'British Political Institutions' and 'The Constitution of Germany', as well as heading his own on 'Comparative Government Problems' and 'Local Government Problems'. By the mid-1930s, Finer was heading courses that tackled emerging ideologies, such as 'The Fascist State in Theory and Practice', working

---

[28] Pulzer 2004.

through fascist critiques of liberalism to understand these new doctrines as they gained traction in society.[29]

Importantly for this nascent department, whose roots had been formed mainly from former Oxford and Cambridge history professors, with barristers-at-law teaching the legal and constitutional classes, this new strand of intellectual enquiry began to evolve into a more recognisably 'modern' faculty of individuals solely investigating political science. On the public administration side of things, William Robson embodied this shift from the law to political science. An administrative lawyer, part of the 'LSE vanguard' of John Griffith and Ivor Jennings who had sharply challenged A. V. Dicey's legal orthodoxy, Robson took First-Class honours in the BSc (Econ.) at the LSE before being called to the Bar by Lincoln's Inn in 1922.[30] Robson continued his education at the School despite the call, completing his PhD in 1924 and taking his post as a lecturer in 1926, where his courses focused on 'The Principles of Administrative Law'.[31] Robson would remain at the LSE until 1962, taking the Chair in Public Administration in 1948 and teaching widely on the intersection of law and emerging political science. His contributions to the discipline include founding the *Political Quarterly* journal in 1930 alongside Leonard Woolf and co-founding the Political Studies Association in 1950, although he struggled alongside Smellie unsuccessfully against the more conservative faculty to name it the Political Science Association.[32]

By the middle of Laski's tenure, the idea of distinct departments within the School was beginning to gain traction. The publication of *The Working Constitution and Practice of the London School of Economics and Political Science* in May of 1937 signalled this shift in thinking, but in practice this changed little of the administration, and was not to be seriously acted upon for another two decades.[33] Disciplines continued to assert their independence as much within the School's walls as they did outside them, carving out new areas of study, but remained 'conveniences rather than barriers' for scholarship.[34]

Laski's great influence over the School was a large part of the reason why both the School and the proto department gained a 'dangerous' and 'socialist' image. The leading Marxist Professor of the era, Ralph Miliband—father of the prominent Labour Party MPs Ed and David Miliband—only lent credence to this image of the School as a radical 'hotbed' of hard-left social thought. Miliband, who arrived at the School in 1941 as an undergraduate and studied as a postgraduate under Laski, taught political science in the Department until 1972. Rodney Barker recalls him as a particularly prominent leading figure during

---

[29] LSE 1935: 205.
[30] Chapman 2004: 163.
[31] Page 2015.
[32] Ibid.
[33] Dahrendorf 1995: 322.
[34] Ibid.: 266.

his time in the department, representing, much like Laski, 'a kind of academic life that, without being unscholarly, was also controversial', retaining some sort of public presence. 'What was extraordinary when I arrived at LSE', he notes, was that:

> people still talked about Harold Laski, the red professor. People would say 'Oh LSE, that is a very left-wing organisation isn't it?', I would say 'No it isn't, you should look at some of the prominent people there: Hayek, Robbins, Oakeshott. A left-wing organisation? Oh come on.' But of course it was all of those things ... There are pluses and minuses about having people in the Department who are known outside the Department. It can often lead to the wrong popular impression of the place.[35]

Indeed, besides Laski and Miliband, there have been relatively few Marxist intellectuals at the School, at least of any repute. Hence, despite its external image cultivated under Laski as a bastion of radical, socialist thought, the ambiguities underlying the fabric of the institution reveal a more conflicted and, in many cases, less ideologically 'pure' faculty than this image would have the casual observer believe. Major leading figures were conservative in nature, such as Lionel Robbins and later Friedrich Hayek in the neighbouring Economics department, which was hardly a separate division within the School until well into Oakeshott's time.[36] The department retained a decidedly historical attitude well into maturity, faintly echoing the classical focus of Oxford and Cambridge under the direction of Oakeshott.[37] In any case, the close association between the department, the School and the socialist movement was to fracture after Laski's death in spectacular fashion, as he was succeeded by the great conservative philosopher Michael Oakeshott in 1950.

Such was Laski's force of personality that it remains a popular myth the department was his creation. No doubt this emerged from his personal prominence and influence on the School's international reputation during its early years. However, it was in fact Oakeshott's arrival at the School that marked the emergence of the Government department in 1950, a fact cemented in 1962 with its formal creation. He was to remain its de facto 'Head' for almost 20 years, retaining the post when the new formal title of departmental 'Convener' swept the School's administrative system from 1962 to 1965. Although H. R. G. Greaves would take over as Convener in 1966, Oakeshott would remain the de facto departmental head until his retirement in 1968, after which regulation changes, begun in the Economics Department, introduced a formal rota system for appointing Heads. From then on, Conveners would usually hold the post for three years. However, he would continue to feature heavily

---

[35] Barker interview 2020.
[36] Alexander interview 2020.
[37] Dahrendorf 1995: 515.

in the Department, and run his famous 'History of Political Thought' course until 1981.[38]

A one-man band, then, the department certainly was not, although its leader was certainly accomplished on many of the instruments they ended up playing. This core of political scientists and public administration lecturers would remain almost a constant until Laski's death, joined by a collection of others in more specialist subjects; the Baron Alexander Felixovich von Meyendorff reprised his classes on topics such as 'Communistic Legislation in Russia' and 'Current Russian Problems' from 1922 until 1934. Ada Wallas continued to lecture occasionally alongside Laski's cohort until her death in 1934, with courses focused on her specialties in literature, specifically the romantic movement in politics, covering 'French Thought in the Eighteenth Century' and 'Political Aspects of the Romantic Movement (1740–1848)'. Hastings Lees-Smith, the prominent parliamentarian and Privy Councillor who had joined as a lecturer in public administration in 1906, remained at the School for the entirety of his career, until his death in 1941. The beginnings of a 'Government Department' were starting to take hold.

The Department and the War

Laski's last years in the department saw the School evacuated to Cambridge in 1939, at the outset of the Second World War. Overseen by the School's Director, Sir Alexander Morris Carr-Saunders, Cambridge's oldest College Peterhouse agreed to house the LSE for the duration of the war, as the Ministry of Works took over the Houghton Street buildings for the war effort. The two institutions could scarcely have been more different; Peterhouse, founded in 1284, was a bastion of pedagogic traditionalism. The School, a vanguard institution of new social sciences and emerging disciplines, had just established itself as the main rival to the 'Cambridge School' of economics and prided itself in its research focus in these emerging fields. It was said at the time that 'Oxford and Cambridge trained people to run the British Empire', whereas the LSE 'trained people to overthrow the British Empire'.[39] At the time, the LSE had just shy of a thousand students, almost half of them women, and with roughly a third of this number in evening students, whose commitment to studies throughout the war was to split the faculty's time between Cambridge and London. As the School's archivist Sue Donnelly notes, by 1944 women made up two-thirds of the total student body of the School, which had risen to 2,151 by the end of the war.[40]

By all accounts, the integration of the LSE into the collegiate life of Peterhouse was a success, and the political scientists were no exception. With a

---

[38] O'Leary interview 2020; Franco & Marsh 2012: 5; Podoksik 2012: xvii.
[39] Hix interview 2020.
[40] Donnelly 2018.

reputation preceding him, Laski's lectures attracted many Cambridge students to listen, and of those LSE faculty who are fondly recalled by students during the 'Cambridge Years', almost half were of the Government department; William Pickles, Hastings Lees-Smith, William Robson and Ivor Jennings, and of course Laski himself, are all remembered as particularly prominent during the years, keeping the emerging discipline of political science alive in the economics-heavy, mathematically minded alcoves of Peterhouse.[41]

The links between this time and the present, with the School having been dispersed by the COVID-19 pandemic halfway through the Lent term in 2020, are hard to ignore. While prone, perhaps, to being compared too superficially, these two epochs in the Department's life share much common ground. Both have involved a great displacement from the Houghton Street campus, the former concentrating it in a single, albeit alien place, the latter scattering its students and professors throughout the world. The department's period at Cambridge was a definite phase in its development, sealed off and isolated from the rest of its life; as Ralf Dahrendorf recalls it, an 'episode', a 'time capsule', for there could not be a London School of Economics and Political Science without London itself.[42] Quite whether this second 'evacuation' will remain a phase, or mark a more fundamental shift in the way the Department approaches education, remains to be seen.

What is certain is that the war had a lasting effect on the character of the department, as it did on the wider world. Even late into the 1950s, former students recall the harrowing impact the war had on former pupils and staff still teaching in the nascent Government department, returning to the bombed-out buildings of central London. Many spoke in private of experiences during the war, among them Keith Panter-Brick, the noted professor of international relations and scholar of area studies, who joined the department in 1950. Captured at Dunkirk after his Lieutenant was shot and killed next to him, Panter-Brick's forced, 300-mile march from Poland to a Stalag labour camp saw him interred in the forced labour camps for the duration of the war. Upon his release, he studied at Keble College, Oxford, before lecturing in Government and International Relations at the LSE. Tales like this, while spoken of in hushed tones, were far from uncommon during the period.[43]

Two of the last permanent appointments during Laski's tenure were to the public administration side of the department, which gained valuable additions in the form of Richard Pear (1947) and Peter Self (1948). Pear returned to the School after the war as a lecturer, having studied politics as an undergraduate there in 1935.[44] Continuing the department's tradition of taking old Oxonians

---

[41] Dahrendorf 1995: 346.
[42] Ibid.: 358.
[43] Alexander interview 2020. Alexander was a student of Panter-Brick.
[44] Childs 1998.

onto the faculty, Self began lecturing on 'Morals and Politics' by the invitation of Laski and Robson in 1948, a class he would continue to run throughout the early Oakeshott years.[45] The famous sociologist, who would succeed Robson to Smellie's chair in 1963, was the leading specialist in cities and urban planning of the period, and was crucial in establishing the MSc in Regional and Urban Planning Studies in what would become the Department of Geography and the Environment.[46] While Self and Pear would split off from the political scientists as the years progressed, they were crucial in helping William Robson found the Greater London Group in 1958, the foremost institution for the study of London government since the 1960s.[47]

On 24 March 1950, Harold Laski passed away after a brief fight with influenza. He had been preparing to speak at a conference held by the LSE on the creation of the Political Studies Association, having laid much of the groundwork the previous year in a series of informal meetings at Paris, Oxford and London.[48] 'Held a prisoner' by his doctor on 22 March, he passed away the evening of the conference's second day, with Robson and Smellie holding the discussions about the 'Political Science Conference' in his stead.[49] Following Laski's death, his friend Felix Frankfurter, the jurist and professor who had first introduced Laski to Holmes, worked hard alongside Lord Chorley to raise funds, mostly from the United States, to purchase the whole of Laski's book collection. The intention was to house it all together in a 'Laski Room' on the LSE campus. After a long fundraising push, the collection was purchased and eventually housed in the rare books room at the renovated LSE library on No. 4, Portugal Street, although the room was not named the Laski Room. This might have been partly due to the School being 'very hard pressed indeed for space' at the time, according to a letter from Mrs Laski regarding the collection. In an *LSE Magazine* article from June 1978, Granville Eastwood called for the Laski Room project to be reignited. He suggested either the Old Theatre or the New Theatre be renamed the Laski Theatre and that the School commission a new volume of Laski's most important works.

In his 30 years in London, Harold Laski had transformed Political Science at the LSE, and indeed in much of the wider world, from an amorphous collection of historians and barristers into one of the central, autonomous disciplines at the School. And although much of the definition that was to be seen in the later departmental structure of the School was clearly lacking, the foundations were there to be built upon.

---

[45] Jones 2016; see also Fig. 2.5.
[46] Hall 1999.
[47] Kochan 2008.
[48] Morris-Jones 1988: 343.
[49] Ibid.

Michael Oakeshott: A Sceptical Mind

Upon his appointment to the School in 1950, Michael Oakeshott may not have been so agreeable to the above description of the Government department. Indeed, in his view, 'the department was very loosely organised' when he got there, and he took steps to unify and expand the beginnings of the faculty cobbled together by Laski over the past 30 years into something more recognisable as a Department of Government.[50] The steps taken by the Cambridge historian to this end would effect a sea change in the character of the department not unlike that of Laski in the 1920s, and would reset the Department's composition for half a century.

On the surface, Laski's successor could not have cast a more different shadow when he took up his Chair that autumn, and a long shadow at that. Although they shared a middle name, this was perhaps the only obvious feature the two men could be said to have held in common, outside their commitment to scholarly investigation. Michael Joseph Oakeshott, a reserved, private man with an individualistic and original outlook on life, had spent his early years reading History at Cambridge before joining the faculty as a Fellow in Philosophy. He later spent the war as an artillery rounds spotter for the intelligence regiment Phantom. His father, Joseph, had been a friend of George Bernard Shaw, was a founding member of the Fabian Society and the LSE, and had written several Fabian pamphlets, as well as delivered Fabian lectures.[51] However, his son had long grown out of any youthful dalliance with socialist ideas. He had become the epitome of a philosophic conservatism which went well beyond politics, and which was to dominate the image of the Department to come.

Oakeshott, who took up the Graham Wallas professorship in Political Science from his post at Nuffield College, Oxford, was a 'very distinctive character' and 'unscrupulous charmer' who 'cast a long shadow'.[52] Counted among the most original minds in 20th-century English political thought, Oakeshott was an enigmatic figure whose work continues to have an impact on philosophy at the School today. However, to many observers, his appointment to the Chair of the School's star professor seemed a little curious, not least because it was doubtful Oakeshott even *believed* that the discipline to which he had been appointed, political science, existed. Oakeshott had been one of the most vocal of the 'conservative' detractors against Laski, Robson and Smellie, seeking to found not a Political Science Association, but a Political Studies Association. He didn't believe in political science as such, and is credited with being perhaps *the* reason why the UK Political Science Association is called the Political Studies Association, with its associated *Political Studies* journal. And so although it was in the name of the institution, the London School of Economics

---

[50] Minogue interview 1988.
[51] O'Sullivan 2014: 473.
[52] O'Leary interview 2020; Charvet interview 2020.

Figure 11: Professor Michael Oakeshott; Credit: LSE Library.

and *Political Science*, Oakeshott 'was going to make damn sure there wasn't a Political Science Department', recalls Professor Brendan O'Leary.[53] To this day, there isn't a Political Science Department at the LSE. There is the Government Department and the International Relations Department, and although they share deep links, they remain distinct and separate entities.

Oakeshott's succession to Laski was therefore not without its controversies, being greeted with 'much dismay' and a flurry of adverse commentary in the more Left-leaning media. R. H. S. Crossman was coruscating in his criticism of the appointment of a 'non-believer' to an influential position in one of the homes of Fabian socialism, writing of 'a cavalier iconoclast, [Oakeshott] marches with his pick-axe into the portals of the School, dedicated by the Webbs' to the scientific study of the improvement of human society; and there he smashes, one by one, the idols with which Laski and Wallas adorned its walls'.[54] In the print media, *The New Statesman* and *Evening Standard* were particularly vocal in their incredulity at Oakeshott's appointment.[55] His arrival heralded a new approach to the study of government at the LSE, one that was to maintain a hold until the last decade of the millennium, on his passing in 1990.

---

[53] O'Leary interview 2020.

[54] Franco 2004: 13.

[55] O'Sullivan 2014:. 477.

His oft-quoted inaugural lecture upon taking his Chair at the School, 'Political Education', set the new tone of this era:

> In political activity ... men sail a boundless and bottomless sea: there is neither harbour for shelter nor floor for anchorage, neither starting-place nor appointed destination. The enterprise is to keep afloat on an even keel; the sea is both friend and enemy; and the seamanship consists in using the resources of a traditional manner of behaviour in order to make a friend of every hostile occasion.[56]

The conservative vein derived from a decidedly liberal philosophy ran throughout his historical works and philosophy of education, and impressed heavily upon the nascent London School at which he arrived. Unsurprisingly, Oakeshott's opinions of his predecessor Laski were rather low, made apparent in his early works on political philosophy from the 1920s and 1930s. Here, he is openly hostile to 'Mr Laski's' various muddled accounts of the state and civil society. These views were crystallised in an interview with Kenneth Minogue towards the end of his life, where Oakeshott remarked that the then-Director of the School, Sir Alexander Carr-Saunders, 'knew a fool when he met one', and there were 'many people at the School he couldn't stand ...', among them 'Laski of course'.[57]

Yet, despite these differences in substance and style, there remains a surprising amount of overlap between the two that links to the founding vision of the School itself. Both Laski and Oakeshott took a comprehensive view of politics and political analysis, drawing little distinction in their work between the various social science subjects such as History, Sociology, Law and International Relations taught at the LSE. This attitude reflects the aims of the School at its inception, an attitude that has somewhat degraded as the institution has grown and departments have delineated their territory within its walls. A particular site of overlap for the pair was constitutional and legal philosophy, although again Laski's more overtly political and practical focus draws a sharp comparison to the abstractness of Oakeshott. Laski's well-known and penetrating accounts of sovereignty and the constitution were matched by Oakeshott's own historical investigations into the nature of human association, both in his *magnum opus, On Human Conduct*, and his famous *Lectures on the History of Political Thought*.[58] In both men, then, despite their differences in the idea of the university and the education one should receive from it, there remained an enduring commitment to the incremental change of society, and the place universities have in helping one understand it.

---

[56] Oakeshott 1991: 60. Given as his inaugural lecture at the LSE in 1951.
[57] Minogue interview 1988.
[58] Oakeshott 2006.

A comparison of the pair's inaugural lectures sheds more light on this continuity thesis. Oakeshott had begun his with a reflection on the department's past, remarking:

> The two former occupants of this Chair, Graham Wallas and Harold Laski, were both men of great distinction; to follow them is an undertaking for which I am ill-prepared. In the first of them, experience and reflection were happily combined to give a reading of politics at once practical and profound; a thinker without a system whose thoughts were nevertheless firmly held together by a thread of honest, patient inquiry; a man who brought his powers of intellect to bear upon the consequence of human behaviour and to whom the reasons of the head and of the heart were alike familiar. In the second, the dry light of intellect was matched with a warm enthusiasm; to the humour of a scholar was joined the temperament of a reformer. It seems but an hour ago that he was dazzling us with the range and readiness of his learning, winning our sympathy by the fearlessness of his advocacy and endearing himself to us by his generosity.[59]

While his remarks covered over an almost visceral disdain for Laski's academic work that peppered his earliest writings, even as early as his successful Fellowship application to Gonville and Caius College, Cambridge, in 1925, Oakeshott's reverence for the man himself speaks volumes to the sort of lecturer he was in practice, and the figure he cut across both the Department and British politics itself.[60] He was described as a force of nature whose words inspired a global generation of students in the nature of political enquiry. One is hard-pressed not to compare these words to Laski's remarks, delivered in the inaugural lecture to the same Chair some 24 years prior:

> I do not want to leave upon you the impression that politics should be studied historically merely for the sake of the history thereby revealed. Our end is to know the causes of things, to attain a perspective whereby the philosophies we adopt may be the richer and truer in substance. I say advisedly the philosophies; the plural noun means that we do not ask in this university the acceptance of any particular creed. My object as the occupant of this chair is not to create a body of disciples who shall go forth to preach the particular and peculiar doctrines I happen to hold. It is rather that the student shall learn the method of testing his own faith against the only solid criterion we know—the experience of mankind. That does not, of course, mean that in the exposition of political philosophy it is one's business to pretend to impartiality. In any case that is

---

[59] Oakeshott 1991: 43–44.
[60] See Oakeshott 2010: 84, 117, 134, 135, 168–169, 203.

impossible; for in the merest selection of material to be considered there is already implied a judgement which reflects, however unconsciously, the inevitable bias that each of us will bring. The teacher's function, as I conceive it, is less to avoid his bias than consciously to assert its presence and to warn his hearers against it; above all, to be open minded about the difficulties it involves and honest in his attempt to meet them. For the greatest thing he can, after all, teach is the lesson of conscious sincerity. More truth is discovered along the road than can be found on any other.[61]

The differences are at once subtle and stark. Laski almost immediately admonishes the historical studies to which Oakeshott was wedded, both by interest and by training. Yet, he affirms many of the principles Oakeshott personally strove to uphold, committed to the creation not of followers, but of *thinkers*. One student of Laski's, none other than B. K. Nehru, once remarked that he had 'reached the opposite conclusions' to those Laski had taught him, to which Laski replied he had only 'taught him how to think'.[62] This, perhaps, is the commonality between the two great professors: a love of teaching not ideals as such, but of ways to think for oneself.

Many have testified to the persuasiveness and impact, not just of Oakeshott's inaugural lecture, but of his teaching style more generally. A student of Oakeshott's at the time, Professor Nicholas Barr, recalls the atmosphere of his lectures:

> I'm a classic economist. I don't understand political theory, but I found these lectures absolutely riveting, riveting as much for the delivery as the content. He was charismatic and again, I'm exaggerating, but sometimes you see a performance of a piece of music you don't understand or a play and you don't understand the language but you can recognise that this is of a stunning quality. And if you didn't understand Michael Oakeshott, he had that ...[63]

Barr's view is mirrored by other students such as Elly Chong, a student at the School later in the period from 1974 to 1975. She recalls Oakeshott to have been the 'strongest influence' on her education personally, not necessarily in 'what he said', 'but the way he said it'.[64] He instilled a great sense in people of the 'importance of context'.[65] Indeed, the influence of R. G. Collingwood and the links to what would be called the Cambridge School approach of historical contextualism on Oakeshott seems to have translated throughout the

---

[61] Laski 1926.
[62] Dahrendorf 1995: 192.
[63] Barr telephone interview 2020.
[64] Chong telephone interview 2020.
[65] Ibid.

Government department's approach during this period, running deep through their methods, if not necessarily the conclusions formed.

The Government department had gained a different sort of leader in the figure of Michael Oakeshott, a leader content to lead from the shadows, rather than proclaim from the frontlines. It was to be his appointments, made under this new philosophy of education, that would guide the development of the department into maturity.

The Changing of the Guard

Understanding the man behind the department during the latter half of this period is crucial, for his historical focus and philosophical scepticism was to reorient the image of the department, both in Britain and within the School itself. Unlike Miliband or Laski, Oakeshott was to preside over a more reserved department not given to maintaining public images or personal followings, although some of his 'disciples' would break with this over the years. George Jones recalls a right-wing 'old boy hold' over the department in the 1950s, with Oakeshott possessing great power over appointments, some of which occurred over a pint in university bars.[66] He was keen to appoint those of a similar philosophical disposition to himself, remoulding the department into one focused on the historical rather than the practical. Figure 12 is a pictorial representation of the department based on the 1950–1951 Calendar. In the year that Oakeshott arrived, courses were split into even divisions between Public Administration, the History of Political Thought, and Political and Social Thought, although a weighting existed towards the latter. Over the years, this balance was to tilt decisively in the favour of 'Oakeshottian' trained political theorists and historians, marginalising the public administration thinkers, and creating a rift between the two.

Upon assuming Laski's role as the informal leader of the political scientists, he began this departmental reconstruction. Elie Kedourie joined in 1953, as a scholar of Middle Eastern politics, having been denied his PhD by the University of Oxford. Kenneth Minogue joined as an assistant lecturer at Oakeshott's invitation in 1956, after completing his evening course BSc (Econ.) at the School, while Maurice Cranston arrived in 1959, again from Oxford.[67] All would follow in Oakeshott's footsteps to head the Department as its 'Convener' across the course of their careers, and cement this move away from Laski under Oakeshott to the study of politics in the Department.

Ideological divisions had always been tolerated within the Department, but conservatism, variously described, was the dominant political discourse well into the 1960s and beyond. During these early Oakeshott years, the division

---

[66] O'Leary interview 2020.
[67] De-La-Noy 2011.

Politics and Public Administration

Political Theory and the ▶

I. The History of Political Thought
Michael Oakeshott

Political Ideas of the
Ancient World, 476 A.D.
Dorothea E. Sharp

English Political ⬥
1715–1815
K.B. Smellie

The History of Political
Ideas, 476–1500
Dorothea E. Sharp   The History of Political
Ideas,1500–1640
M. Oakeshott

English P◀
Thought
1815–193⬥
H.R.G. Gr◀

The History of
Political Ideas,
1640–1715
J.W.N. Watkins

III. Political and Social T▶
Graduate Courses

Public Administration

Political Thought
K.B. Smellie

German Political
Thought
Friedrich Darmstaedte◀

The Government
of Great Britain
W.A. Robson   Commonwealth
Relations
W.H. Morris-Jones

Introduction
to Politics
K.B. Smellie   The Government
of France
W. Pickles

The Government of the
United States of America
R.H. Pear

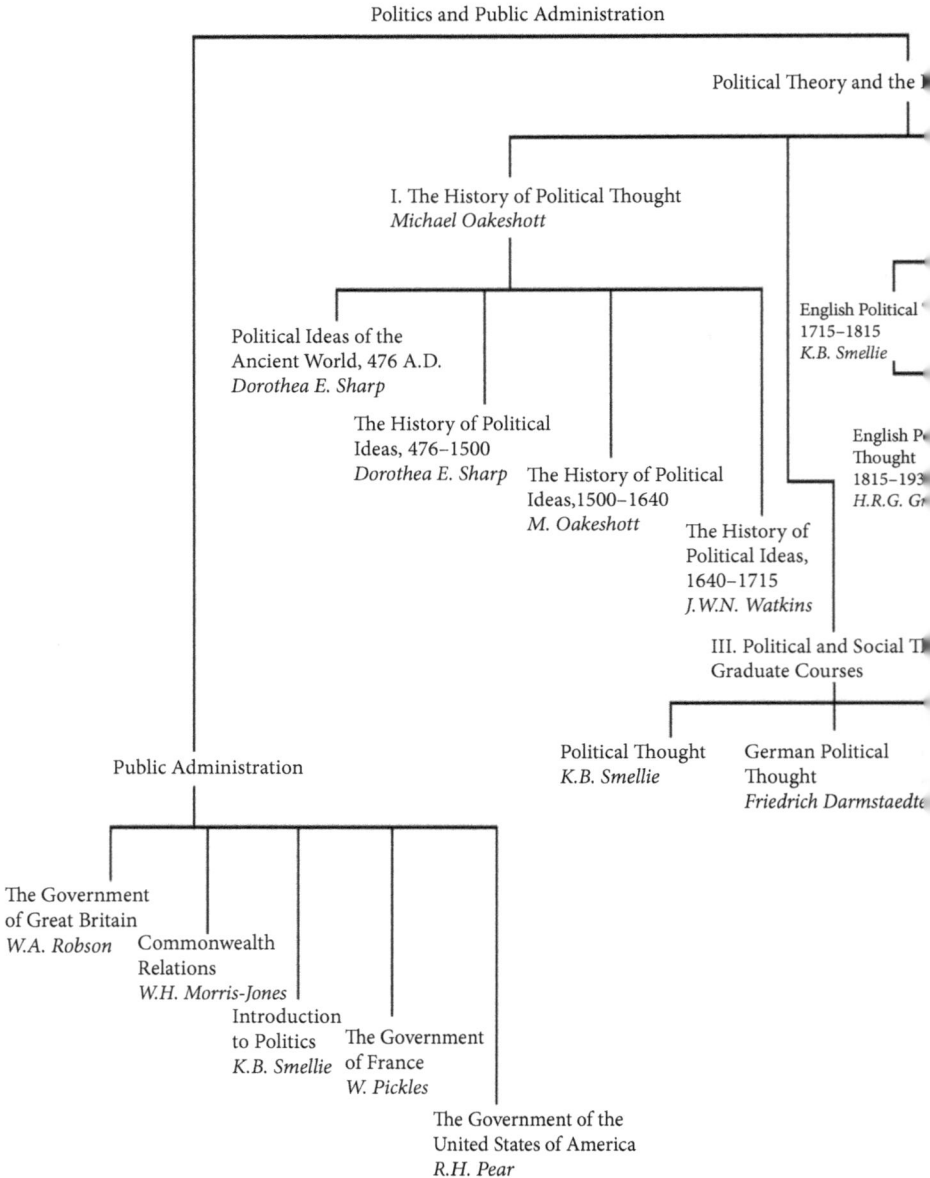

Figure 12: The London School of Economics and Political Science Faculty of
Government, Calendar for the Fifty-Sixth Session, 1950–51 (London, 1950);
Credit: Mapping created by D. Skeffington.

cal Thought

II. Social and Political Thought
K.B. Smellie

Political Thought 1715–1815
les and R. Miliband

German Political
Thought since 1780
H.S. Reiss

French Political Thought,
1815–1939
W. Pickles

Politics and Social Theory
K.B. Smellie

Morals and Politics
P.J.O. Self

American Political Ideas,
1779–1939
R.H. Pear

Philosophy and Politics
J.W.N. Watkins

Marxism and Communism
S.K. Panter-Brick

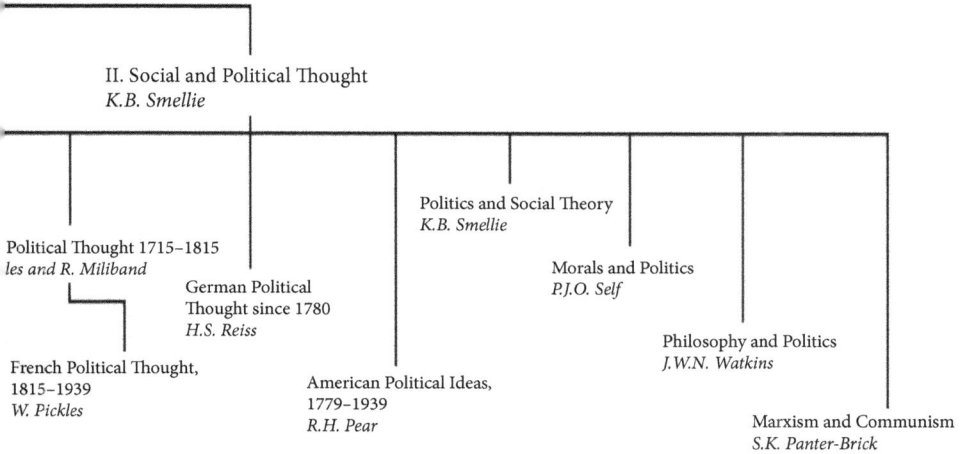

vative Thought
urke
orris-Jones

between Political Science and Public Administration began to grow, with the old grouping of Peter Self and William Robson starting to go their own way, splitting off from the new cohort of 'Oakeshottians'.[68] A prominent force in their day alongside the 'Peterhouse Right' of Cambridge, the College to which the Department had evacuated during the War, these Oakeshottians were an ill-defined grouping of academics embodying a certain sceptical outlook towards politics and political education, rather than a well-defined 'ideological' intellectual movement. Indeed, such a position would have been antithetical to Oakeshott's worldview. This was encapsulated best by Minogue, who was said to hold an 'Oakeshottian hatred' of ideological shibboleths.[69]

A dislike of any sort of 'universalist' philosophy would define Oakeshott's work, and the Department he ran, for almost half a century. Oakeshott's suspicion of Fabianism was that it was Baconian in inspiration, and that the source of its pragmatic, gradualist approach was derived from Bacon's *New Atlantis*, published in 1624, of the technological society ruled by scientific experts. The 'ends' were everything to the Fabians and 'means' were less important so long as the goals of collectivism were achieved. This attitude could be taken to explain the Webbs' susceptibility to praise Soviet communism despite the anti-democratic nature of the Bolsheviks, and the limits to personal freedom and liberty in the form of restrictions on freedom of expression and speech. Thus, even moderate and 'democratic' socialism could not be trusted. So it was that as late as 1981 the *Financial Times* described the Government Department at the LSE as 'the most right-wing political science department in the Western World', with distinctive voices like Oakeshott, Minogue and Middle-East scholar Elie Kedourie hovering in the background of its image.[70] And while this description wasn't quite true, due to the influence of the 'Old Fabians' in both British politics and public policy and administration, Oakeshott's philosophers and historians certainly made their mark, both on the Department's image and the School as a whole.[71]

Elie Kedourie was the first to signal this shift, a leading if quiet mind in the department of Government, and a vociferous critic of the post-colonial orthodoxy dominating his field. He had studied under Laski as an undergraduate at the School in 1950, the year before his death, and had made an impression on both him and K. B. Smellie in his undergraduate work.[72] A major but somewhat forgotten scholar in the emerging discipline of Middle Eastern Studies, Kedourie was a founder and editor of the journal of the same name in 1964, a post he would remain at throughout his career. He was fiercely independent, railing against the dominating, Orientalist accounts of his field—an attitude

---

[68]   Dahrendorf 1995: 418.
[69]   O'Leary interview 2020.
[70]   Ibid.
[71]   Ibid.
[72]   Beattie 1998: 110.

that cost him his doctorate in Oxford—and refusing to bring his thesis into line with the 'misconceptions' of his examiner, the leading Middle Eastern scholar of the day.[73] Kedourie's main criticisms centred on the mismanagement of the Ottoman Empire by the British, accusing them of fomenting discord and war by carving the old stable empire up into

> artificial entities in accordance with their imperial interests and in complete disregard of local yearning for political unity. By way of doing so, the British (allegedly) duped the naive and well-intentioned Arab nationalist movement into a revolt against its Ottoman suzerain, only to cheat it of its fruits and break the historical unity of a predominantly Arab area.[74]

Reflecting on her husband's work, Sylvia Kedourie (herself an eminent scholar of the Middle East), concludes: 'As a historian of the Middle East, he completely changed the approach to the subject. His interpretation, revolutionary as it was, has now become so accepted that people can no longer appreciate how novel his ideas were when he started writing in the 1950s.'[75] Although a conservative in nature, Kedourie was, like Oakeshott, some distance from a 'conservative' caricature. He went through considerable effort to distance conservatism from the political 'right', believing that conservatism-proper consisted of a scepticism about what politics could reasonably achieve.

Leonard Schapiro, the leading professor of Soviet politics and totalitarianism in the Department, joined two years later in 1955, expanding the range of the faculty significantly in these areas. Drawn away from the London Bar by the collaborative efforts of Robson and Oakeshott, where he had practised both before and after the war, Schapiro headed a renewed effort to expand the Department's specialisation in Russian politics, taking up where Baron von Meyendorff had left off. Remembered fondly for his lecturing style, Schapiro was swiftly appointed professor in 1963, became Convenor after H. R. G. Greaves in 1969 and stayed on as professor until his retirement in 1975.[76]

Schapiro was joined the following year by Kenneth Minogue, another central and unusually outspoken member of the Oakeshottian cohort. An Australian philosopher with an 'intense passion for archaic English conservatism', combined with a libertarian political philosophy, Minogue was one of few in the Department who took a political stance. Perhaps Oakeshott's 'chief disciple', Minogue was an advocate of putting his more abstract philosophy into practice. He was 'a founding member of the Bruges group', a right-wing think tank promoting the merits of independence from the European Union, whose first

---

[73] Karsh 1999: 704–706.

[74] Ibid.: 706.

[75] Kedourie 2005: 647.

[76] Reddaway 1975: 13; Camfield 2016; Shukman 2004.

Honorary President was Margaret Thatcher, and one of the few Oakeshottians to become involved in policymaking.[77] Similar in his libertarian leanings
to Minogue, which grew progressively more right-wing over his time in the
Department, was Maurice Cranston. A historian and philosopher appointed
by Oakeshott in 1959, Cranston would continue to teach until 1985 on Political
Science and Philosophy, lecturing on the history of political thought. Cranston
would enjoy considerably more success as a political biographer than he would
as a philosopher. His study of the life of John Locke, published in 1957, is still
considered the 'definitive' study of the life of this great political philosopher,
matched by others of a similar calibre on Sartre and Rousseau throughout
his career.[78]

This group of philosophers and historians, moulded in Oakeshott's image,
was a clear divergence from Laski's band of administrative professionals.
But was this conservative image of the young Government Department a clean
break with the Fabian traditions of the School's founders? Anne Phillips, the
current holder of Graham Wallas's Chair at the School, helpfully interrogates
this idea of an Oakeshottian/non-Oakeshottian split in the Department. She
argues these thinkers were often not divided along political lines *per se*, but by
differing views concerning the nature of political enquiry itself. It was a split
between those 'who are very committed to the study of politics being made
as precise and scientific as possible' and 'those who think the study of politics
should be addressing big questions that can't and don't actually lend themselves
to that degree of precision'. Such enquiries could dominate either the left or the
right of the political spectrum, although Phillips sees no necessary tension in
the Department along conservative or socialist lines as such.[79] And although
Oakeshott has often been perceived as a right-wing thinker, with Perry Anderson counting him among the 'intransigent right' of Hayek, Schmitt and Strauss,
his influence in mainstream liberal and even centre left-wing political theory
has steadily grown since his death, particularly in constitutional thought. That
is not to say that the Department during this period was free of such intransigent right-wing thinkers, and its leanings were certainly to the right of centre even in 1965.[80] Rather that, as under Laski, its external image was more
influenced by the outspoken members of this cohort, such as Minogue. If there
was a difference, it was in temperament and style of teaching, rather than any
deeply ingrained ideological rift; Laski 'the orator' versus Oakeshott 'the conversationalist', as Dahrendorf so eloquently put it.[81]

---

[77] O'Leary interview 2020.
[78] De-La-Noy 2011; Burns 1995.
[79] Phillips telephone interview 2020.
[80] Charvet interview 2020.
[81] Dahrendorf 1995: 368.

The Department under Oakeshott

The Government Department under Oakeshott was 'a large one, and grew larger during his tenure', from 12 members on his arrival—already the largest in the country—to 30 when he left.[82] Patrick Dunleavy recalls it as a time dominated by a philosophical rather than practical outlook, fitting with Oakeshott's own views of politics.[83] The logic underpinning Oakeshott's disdain for 'political science' was also to influence the administration of the day-to-day affairs. He insisted that the Department should have a 'Convener' and not a 'Head'; a first-among-equals position whose job was convening their colleagues in discussion, rather than through 'top-down planning' or dictation. Oakeshott's passionate and embodied defence of the LSE as this 'community of scholars', rather than a business-like factory of trained graduates, acknowledges a tension that persists to this day in the Department—the extent to which university education should be about training for jobs rather than a broader liberal education. Established as a vocational business school with a specific remit to encourage debate, discussion and critical thinking among a new class of professional governmental administrators, the LSE was lent academic credentials by joining the University of London in 1900. As George Jones would later recognise, this issue remains a key question in the identity and purpose of the Department as an institution in British and global education.

Despite the political divisions raised by his appointment and his old-fashioned style, writing as he did everything in longhand, Oakeshott was a 'brilliant administrator' and 'spread a spirit of collegiality' during his tenure as Convener. He devoted his time not to writing books, nor to 'preaching conservatism as Laski had done socialism', but to promoting academic work and standards.[84] He was, as Parekh notes, not always a major intellectual presence at the School by nature, but his hand was felt everywhere in the manner in which he guided the Department, led by a 'strong sense of his own authority' in the role, coupled with a 'keen appreciation of what was required for the maintenance of amicable relations amongst his colleagues'.[85] In an interview with Ken Minogue, towards the end of his life, Oakeshott paints a picture of himself as rather removed from the politics of the university, which he explicitly notes he loathed, committed instead to the delivery and running of the courses as best he could. He seems driven by his devotion to his subjects and his intellectual 'adventuring'. There were only a few departmental meetings per year, but they did not last long; Oakeshott generally got his own way at departmental

---

[82] Kedourie 1998: 6; Johnson 1991: 410; see Fig. I, *The London School of Economics and Political Science Department of Government, 1950–1951.*

[83] Dunleavy interview 2019.

[84] *The Times*, Saturday, 22 December 1990.

[85] Parekh 1999: 101; Johnson 1991: 411.

meetings and School committees.[86] And, while this perhaps misses some 'flashes of turmoil; adversarial encounters with colleagues and authorities' that are common to all institutions, Oakeshott's time at the helm of the Department seems to be recalled with general warmth.

While Oakeshott's leadership and personal qualities are given subtle praise during this time, the same cannot be said for its formal research profile, which would suffer on his watch. The Department consistently performed poorly when Research Assessment Exercises were introduced towards the end of his association with the School in the late 1980s, which comes as no surprise to those aware of Oakeshott's approach to education.[87] On the contrary, it correlates rather well with his final work, *The Voice of Liberal Learning*, published in 1989, where he extols the virtues of subtle, comprehensive education against the sensibilities of 'gaining knowledge' for practical use. Research, or the idea that you would 'waste your time writing fresh articles or accumulating knowledge, or the notion of a frontier of knowledge', were indeed 'bizarre notions' for Oakeshottians.[88] Their focus was on the manner in which one was taught, as well as the manner one developed, rather than any particular 'skill' as such.

Several professors, past and present, have recalled these divisions within the Department, before the Oakeshottian cohort of academics began to be eclipsed. The re-emergence of public policy and political science to challenge the hitherto dominant field of political philosophy, as well as public administration, and British colonial administration, under the tutelage and leadership of the charismatic Oakeshott, was the work of many years, but proved to be irresistible. This evolution of the Department went alongside a clearer sense of its identity, largely a consequence of Departmental restructuring during the period. The emergence of a more professional approach has been remarked on by several colleagues—an academic community more engaged in research and, like much of academia in the second half of the 20th century, tending towards specialisation—although this wasn't to take full effect until well after Oakeshott's association ended.[89] However, even towards the end of the period in 1964, Ken Minogue remarked on the deficiencies of the course content:

> The courses are mostly too broad—the conflict between breadth and depth is virtually insoluble. One just has to strike a compromise. The objection to broad courses is that the broader they are, the more dishonesty they involve. Students have no alternative but to learn off second-or-third-hand judgments, and pass them off as their own.[90]

---

[86]   Minogue 2002: 69.
[87]   See Oakeshott 2001, particularly Timothy Fuller's Introduction, 'The idea of a university' and 'Learning and teaching'.
[88]   O'Leary interview 2020.
[89]   In interviews, George Jones and Patrick Dunleavy gave particular emphasis to specialisation.
[90]   'Mr. Ken Minogue … Frankly Speaking', *The Beaver*, 7 May 1964.

This is, perhaps, a natural tension in the study of the social sciences and the humanities; a balance to be struck between breadth and depth, which is inherent in the process of learning the subject itself.

The impact of location on the identity of the Department, however, remained much the same as it had even prior to Laski. Teaching was still conducted across the campus buildings, with a focus on the Old Building, but the Government Department had no one place it could call home. Offices were still shared by academics of all stripes within the School, as John Charvet recalls, who joined at Oakeshott's invitation in 1965;[91] he himself shared office space with a law scholar, fostering the interdisciplinary culture the Founders had embraced and envisioned.[92] However, by 1962, the discussions first mooted by the School's Constitution Committee in 1937 came to fruition, and the Department of Government was formally established alongside a host of others that had attained relative independence over the 1940s.[93] Oakeshott took his place as the first Convener of the Department, a title that was to remain in use until 2007. The one-man band had finally emerged from its ad hoc trappings and garnered an identity of its own.

Conclusion

While the Oakeshottians maintained their progenitor's distance from the practical world of political life, they nevertheless kept a steady influence on it through their works. Oakeshott's noted influence on history and philosophy was cemented by his early analysis of fascism, communism and the other *Social and Political Doctrines of Contemporary Europe* in his 1939 work of the same name. His impact on Hobbes' scholarship has been recognised as significant and original by leading figures in liberal political thought, such as the Cambridge School historians Quentin Skinner and Noel Malcolm. Two eminent contemporary professors of law at the School, Martin Loughlin and Thomas Poole, continue to draw on and critique Oakeshott's later and most significant works, *On Human Conduct* and *On History*, with reference to the legal philosophy for their own accounts of public and constitutional law to this day, as do the wider circles of legal academia in which they run.[94] Indeed, his work continues to be taught at the LSE on courses in the 'History of Political Thought', on the very same MSc programme he founded some half a century ago.[95]

---

[91] Grant 2012: 32.

[92] Charvet interview 2020.

[93] Dahrendorf 1995: 437.

[94] See Poole & Dyzenhaus 2017; Loughlin 1992: 63–83; Loughlin 2004: 153–163; see also Gerencser 2012.

[95] 'Advanced Study of Key Political Thinkers: Hobbes', course on the MSc in Political Theory at the LSE 2019–2020, run by Dr. Signy Gutnick-Allen; see also Malcolm 2012. A view shared by former and current professors, taken from interviews with Professors John Charvet, Anne Phillips and Brendan O'Leary.

Although Elie Kedourie has remained a marginal figure in wider political studies, and is remembered as a fairly ineffectual lecturer, his work has been recognised in hindsight as important and path-breaking on Middle Eastern scholarship, and alongside Cranston's political biographies forms some of the Department's stellar scholarship during the period.[96] Yet, the Department's main strength during the early Oakeshottian years, Kedourie aside, seems to have been that of its teaching style, developed through a solid grouping of professors drawn as much by Oakeshott's historical leanings as they were by his style of pedagogy.

By 1965, then, the Department had radically shifted its image, through the golden formative Laski years and back again to the liberal right of Oakeshott's new cohort. It had, by now, formally *become* the Department of Government, even if its roots had been established decades before, and was maturing into a major entity within the School. Divisions remained between the old public administration appointees lingering from Laski's tenure and this new guard, historical and philosophical, with a focus not so much on research as understanding. These divisions were to come to a head not long after, during the days of the *soixante-huitards*, and the student protests of May 1968. And it is to this tumultuous period that we now turn.

References

Abse, J (ed.) 1977 *My LSE*. London: Robson Books.

Beattie, A 1998 Elie Kedourie's philosophical history. In: Kedourie, S, *Elie Kedourie CBE, FBA, 1926–1992: History, philosophy, politics*. London. Frank Cass Press.

Burns, J H 1995 *Libera communitas*: The problem of constituent power. *The Maurice Cranston Memorial Lecture*. Shaw Lecture Theatre, LSE.

Camfield, G 2016 The beginnings of the Russian collection at LSE, *LSE Blogs*, 22 June. Available at https://blogs.lse.ac.uk/lsehistory/2016/06/22/the-russian-collection-at-lse-library/#:~:text=Collection%20at%20LSE-,The%20beginnings%20of%20the%20Russian%20Collection%20at%20LSE,Science%2C%20opened%20in%20November%201896.&text=At%20LSE%20this%20was%20stimulated,and%20broadsheets%20to%20the%20Library.

Chapman, R A 2004 *The Civil Service Commission, 1855–1991: A bureau biography*. London: Routledge.

Childs, D 1998 Obituary: Professor Richard Pear, *The Independent*, 4 March. Available at https://www.independent.co.uk/life-style/obituary-professor-richard-pear-1148222.html.

---

[96] Matravers telephone interview 2020.

Dahrendorf, R 1995 *A history of the London School of Economics and Political Science, 1895–1995.* Oxford: Oxford University Press.

De-La-Noy, M 2011 Obituary: Professor Maurice Cranston. *The Independent,* 20 October. Available at https://www.independent.co.uk/news/people /obituary-professor-maurice-cranston-1502904.html.

de Wolfe Howe, M (ed.) 1953 *Holmes-Laski letters: The correspondence of Mr Justice Holmes and Harold J. Laski, 1916–1935.* London: Harvard University Press.

Donnelly, S 2015 LSE's almost alumnus—John Fitzgerald Kennedy (1917– 1963), *LSE Blogs,* 25 November. Available at https://blogs.lse.ac.uk/lsehistory /2015/11/25/the-almost-alumnus-john-fitzgerald-kennedy-1917–1963/.

Donnelly, S 2018 Evacuation to Cambridge. *LSE Blogs,* 21 February. Available at https://blogs.lse.ac.uk/lsehistory/2018/02/21/evacuation-to-cambridge/.

Eliot, T S 2016 *The letters of T. S. Eliot,* Vol. 6: *1932–1933.* London: Faber & Faber.

Franco, P 2004 *Michael Oakeshott: An introduction.* Yale, CT: Yale University Press.

Franco, P and **Marsh, L** (eds.) 2012 *A companion to Michael Oakeshott.* Pennsylvania, PA: Pennsylvania State University Press.

Gerencser, S 2012 Oakeshott on law. In: Franco, P and Marsh, L (eds.), *A companion to Michael Oakeshott.* Pennsylvania, PA: Pennsylvania State University Press.

Grant, R 2012 The pursuit of intimacy. In: Franco, P and Marsh, L (eds.), *A companion to Michael Oakeshott.* Pennsylvania, PA: Pennsylvania State University Press.

Hall, P 1999 Obituary: Professor Peter Self. *The Independent,* 13 April. Available at https://www.independent.co.uk/arts-entertainment/obituary-professor -peter-self-1087099.html.

Johnson, N 1991 *Proceedings from the British Academy, 1991 lectures and memoirs.* Oxford: Oxford University Press.

Jones, G 2016 From the archive: George Jones on Peter Self at the LSE, *LSE Blogs,* 7 January. Available at https://blogs.lse.ac.uk/lsehistory/2016/01/07 /from-the-archives-george-jones-on-peter-self-at-lse/.

Karsh, E 1999 Elie Kedourie: Forgotten iconoclast. *International History Review,* 21(3): 704–714.

Kedourie, E 1998 Michael Oakeshott, a Colleague's view. *Middle Eastern Studies,* 33(5): 5–7.

Kedourie, S 2005 Aspects of Elie Kedourie's work. *Middle Eastern Studies,* 41(5): 635–648.

Kochan, B 2008 *London government 50 years of debate: The contribution of LSE's Greater London Group.* LSE London Development Workshops, London School of Economics and Political Science, London, UK.

Krammick, I and **Sheerman, B** 1993 *Harold Laski: A life on the left.* London: Allen Lane.

Laski, H 1919 *The Authority of the modern state*. Yale, CT: Yale University Press.

Laski, H 1921 *The foundations of sovereignty and other essays*. New York: Harcourt Brace & Co.

Laski, H 1926 On the study of politics: An inaugural lecture delivered at the London School of Economics and Political Science. Archives Special JA/30.

Laski, H 2015 *Reflections on the constitution*. Oxford: Routledge.

Loughlin, M 1992 *Public law and political theory*. Oxford: Oxford University Press.

Loughlin, M 2004 *The idea of public law*. Oxford: Oxford University Press.

LSE 1935 *The London School of Economics and Political Science, University of London, Calendar for the forty-first session*. London: London School of Economics and Political Science, 1935–36.

LSE Library n.d. LSE connections with the Indian subcontinent. Available at https://www.lse.ac.uk/library/assets/documents/LSE-connections-with -the-Indian-Subcontinent-timeline.pdf.

Malcolm, N 2012 Oakeshott and Hobbes. In Franco, P and Marsh, L (eds.), *A companion to Michael Oakeshott*. Pennsylvania, PA: Pennsylvania State University Press.

Minogue, K 2002 Michael Oakeshott as a character. *Society*, 39(March/April): 66–70.

Morris-Jones, W H 1988 Professor K. B. Smellie. *Political Studies Association*, 36: 341–344.

Newman, M 1993 *Harold Laski: A political biography*. London: Springer.

Oakeshott, M 1991 *Rationalism in politics: And other essays*. Indianapolis, IN: Liberty Fund Inc.

Oakeshott, M 2001 *The voice of liberal learning*. Carmel, IN: Liberty Fund Inc.

Oakeshott, M 2006 *Lectures on the history of political thought*. Exeter: Imprint Academic.

Oakeshott, M 2010 *Early political writings, 1925–1930*. Exeter: Imprint Academic.

Orwell, G 2013 *Politics and the English language*. London: Penguin.

O'Sullivan, L 2014 Michael Oakeshott and the left. *Journal of the History of Ideas*, 75(3): 471–492.

Page, E 2015 William Robson and the Greater London Group at LSE, *LSE Blogs*, 13 May. Available at https://blogs.lse.ac.uk/lsehistory/2015/05/13/william -robson-and-the-greater-london-group-at-lse/.

Parekh, B 1999 Remembering Michael Oakeshott. *Cambridge Review*, 112(2314): 101.

Podoksik, E 2012 *The Cambridge companion to Michael Oakeshott*. Cambridge. Cambridge University Press.

Poole, T and **Dyzenhaus, D** 2017 *Law, liberty and state; Oakeshott, Hayek and Schmitt on the rule of law*. Cambridge: Cambridge University Press.

Pulzer, P 2004 Finer, Samuel Edward (1915–1993), political scientist. *Oxford Dictionary of National Biography*, 23 September.

Rand, A and **Peikoff, L** 1999 *The journals of Ayn Rand*. London: Penguin.

Reddaway, P 1975 *LSE Magazine*, No. 49, June.

Schmitt, S 2014 *Dictatorship*. Cambridge. Polity Press.

Shukman, H 2004 Schapiro, Leonard Bertram (1908–1983), historian and barrister. *Oxford Dictionary of National Biography*.

Shearhard, S 2014 *The passionate economist: How Brian Abel-Smith shaped global health and social welfare*. Bristol: Bristol University Press.

Interviews

Alexander, Richard, interview by Hilke Gudel, 17 February 2020.

Barker, Rodney, interview by Hilke Gudel, 10 February 2020.

Barr, Nicholas, telephone interview by Hilke Gudel, 16 April 2020.

Charvet, John, interview by Sara Luxmore, 18 February 2020.

Chong, Elly, telephone interview by Hilke Gudel, 5 February 2020.

Dunleavy, Patrick, interview by C Schonhardt-Bailey, 6 December 2019.

Hix, Simon, interview by Hilke Gudel, 13 February 2020.

Matravers, Matt, telephone interview by Hilke Gudel, 22 May 2020.

Minogue, Kenneth, interview between Professor Kenneth Minogue and Professor Michael Oakeshott, 1988.

O'Leary, Brendan, interview by Hilke Gudel, 3 February 2020.

Phillips, Anne, telephone interview by Hilke Gudel, 23 March 2020.

CHAPTER 3

A Place for Rebels?

The Limbo Years, 1966–1989

Lukasz Kremky, Ebla Bohmer and Daniel Skeffington

Introduction

The period spanning the mid-1960s to the late 1980s was a time of profound change for the Government Department at the LSE. While it had recently matured into a fully-fledged division within the School under Oakeshott's leadership, intra-departmental friction had already started to surface. Between 1966 and 1969, divisions were triggered by a series of student protests at the LSE that made national and international headlines. The emergence of a student 'New Left' turned the university campus into a flashpoint of political activism, and students were determined to capture the high ground. It was a time of youth activism and the rise of counterculture, marked by a propensity for direct action against established authorities.

The protests began as a campaign against the appointment of the new LSE Director, Dr. Walter Adams, but as time went by students took to the streets to protest a number of issues, leaving deep scars on the relationship between students and staff. Tensions were high: as Lord Dahrendorf described it, it was 'a less happy age for the social sciences and their practitioners'[1]—perhaps even

---

[1] Dahrendorf 1995: 445.

How to cite this book chapter:
Kremky, L., Bohmer, E. and Skeffington, D. 2021. A Place for Rebels? The Limbo Years, 1966–1989. In: Schonhardt-Bailey, C. and Bannerman, G. (eds.) *Political Science at the LSE: A History of the Department of Government, from the Webbs to COVID*. Pp. 87–110. London: Ubiquity Press. DOI: https://doi.org/10.5334/bcn.d. License: CC-BY-NC

the unhappiest years in the history of the LSE. The protests also shaped the reputation of both the School and the Department. The LSE was now to be popularly known as a 'School for Rebels', a breeding ground for far-left radical thought—a perception that was in reality far from the truth considering the myriad of scholars from different ends of the political spectrum housed by the Government Department in the late 1960s.[2]

At the turn of the decade, a clear intellectual divide had solidified in the Department. Oakeshott retired in 1968, but the two camps—the 'Oakeshottians' versus the 'non-Oakeshottians'—endured into the following decade. The 1970s was a period characterised by division, mediocrity and dissonance; the two groups disagreed vigorously on their approaches to the study of politics, with the Department consequently lacking a cohesive vision or unified strategy. Its glory days under Laski and Oakeshott had reached an end, and it now attempted to reorient itself amid a string of significant and tumultuous changes. By the 1980s, policies enacted under the Thatcher Government helped unify and professionalise the Department, although these would not truly come to fruition until this cohort came to prominence in the early 1990s. And, while these reforms were met with criticism from some in the Department, most notably Elie Kedourie, the introduction of new formal administrative structures, including the Research Assessment frameworks, marked the beginning of a more modern, more professional and ever-growing Government Department.

Revolution is in the Air

The 1960s marked a time of inchoate global disruption, with a wave of student protests erupting around the world. They began at the University of California, Berkeley, where students began campaigning for the civil rights movement in 1964. By 1968, this radical spark had reached academic institutions in Europe. On 22 March 1968, student revolutionaries at the University of Nanterre had occupied the university's administration building, protesting male–female dormitory restrictions.[3] By early May of the same year, protests erupted at Sorbonne University. What at first seemed like innocuous student strikes had quickly transformed into nationwide civil unrest. Between 2 May and 23 June 1968, 11 million *soixante-huitards* stormed the streets of Paris with barricades and tear gas. Workers were demanding higher wages and occupied factories across France, while students continued to violently push for greater levels of student self-government and autonomy in university administration. The impulses flowing from the events in France provided impetus for a revolutionary movement in the United Kingdom. Between 1968 and 1969, the universities of

---

[2] Dahrendorf 1995: 456.
[3] Crouzet 1969: 332.

Essex, Hull, Birmingham, Warwick, the LSE and the Hornsey College of Art saw a spike in campus revolts and occupations, with some institutions—including the LSE—temporarily closing. The student protests at the School undoubtedly garnered the most media attention in the United Kingdom, and not with favourable connotations. With headlines such as 'Rebellion at the School for Rebels',[4] the LSE became notorious as the United Kingdom's hotspot for delinquency and political radicalism—an image from which the School would not easily recover.

An account of the events leading up to and during the student protests is necessary to understand the context of the Government Department at the time. The series of disturbances which occurred from 1966 to 1969 had a profound impact, most notably on relations between students and staff. The troubles at LSE began with the appointment of a new LSE Director. In the summer of 1965, a Selection Committee was established with the mandate of selecting a new School Director to replace the retiring Sydney Caine from October 1967. The Committee—which included two professors from the Government Department, Michael Oakeshott and Leonard Schapiro[5]—spent almost a year sifting through potential candidates, before settling on Sir Walter Adams.

The appointment of Adams led to historic turbulence on the LSE campus. Students began by condemning Adams's administrative record, particularly his passivity during Rhodesia's illegal unilateral declaration of independence (UDI). Adams had previously served as the Secretary of the LSE in 1938, but joined the Foreign Office during the war as Assistant Deputy Director-General of the Political Intelligence Department.[6] After the war, he became Secretary of the Inter-University Council for Higher Education in the Colonies, a position he held from 1946 to 1955, before being appointed the Principal of the College of Rhodesia and Nyasaland. A number of students, who were in strong opposition to Adams', association with the racist regime of Ian Smith in Rhodesia,[7] felt excluded from his appointment process.[8] On 19 August 1966, *Private Eye* released a comment on Walter Adams and Rhodesia, stating that: 'No one would call him a racist. But he has exhibited a constant willingness to compromise, and accept the status quo, even in an unconstitutional de facto regime.'[9] In October 1966, the LSE Socialist Society published a 20-page exposé on Adams in the *Agitator*, entitled *LSE's New Director: A Report on Walter Adams*, which lambasted Adams for failing to oppose the UDI.[10] The exposé concluded with a

---

[4] Dahrendorf 1995: 456; Headland interview 2020.
[5] Dahrendorf 1995: 445.
[6] No author 1967: 312.
[7] Donnelly 2019b.
[8] LSE 2019.
[9] Dahrendorf 1995: 447.
[10] London School of Economics Students 1966, (as quoted in Dahrendorf 1995: 448).

Figure 13: Free LSE Banner; Credit: The Beaver, 1966.

biting remark, that Adams is 'a Principal unprepared to defend the freedom of his staff and students' and was therefore 'not a suitable person to be in charge of any centre of higher education', especially 'a multi-racial college like L.S.E.'. While the authors could not have predicted it, this essay would help foment a conflict brewing within the Government Department, igniting the troubles that were to plague the School for several years to come.

David Adelstein, then-President of the LSE Students' Union, sent a copy of the pamphlet to the Chairman of the Court of Governors, Lord Bridges, enquiring whether the Selection Committee was aware of Adams's background when they made the decision that Adams was eminently suitable to become the next LSE Director. In his response, Bridges noted that 'appointments were confidential and that there would be no public debate on the merits of the case'.[11] Lord Bridges wrote to *The Times* on 25 October claiming it would be inappropriate to enquire into Adams's role in Rhodesia as this would mean meddling in the internal affairs of another institution.[12] Adelstein, although advised not to write to the press about School matters without the permission of the Director, wrote to *The Times* in response to the letter published by Lord Bridges: 'it is difficult to understand how one can avoid discussing a man's record as an administrator in one college when he is being considering for the post as Director in another'.[13] Adelstein was inclined to write as a private citizen, and not in his official capacity as President of the SU, but the School reacted swiftly to his public letter.[14] Ultimately, the Board of Discipline decided not to impose

---

[11]   Ibid.: 449.
[12]   Donnelly 2019b.
[13]   Ibid.
[14]   Dahrendorf 1995: 449.

a penalty on Adelstein, but tensions between the administration and students continued to soar.

The campaign against Adams resumed in the Lent term of 1967. A number of students were dissatisfied with how the administration had handled the situation thus far. As a student wrote in *The Beaver*: 'if the Adams affair is not ventilated, there will be a loss of confidence in the democracy of the LSE'.[15] In response, students planned a sit-in in the Old Theatre, and on 31 January began gathering in the foyer of the Old Building. An off-duty porter, Edward Poole, arrived at the scene to help his colleagues control the crowd, yet amid the confusion Poole suffered a heart attack and tragically died. Although he had an existing heart condition and there was no suggestion that he had been directly assaulted, the death rocked the School, which closed that day in response. The Board of Discipline, chaired by Lord Bridges, decided to take disciplinary action against Bloom, Adelstein and four other members of the Student Council. While the four members of the Student Council were exonerated, Bloom and Adelstein were both found guilty of disobeying the instruction forbidding the use of the Old Theatre for a meeting, and subsequently suspended until the end of the summer. In response, students began a boycott of lectures to demand that suspensions for Bloom and Adelstein be lifted, escalating tensions further.

In what was described as the 'first major student strike [the UK] has known',[16] 800 students occupied the Old Building during a sit-in which lasted eight days in March 1967 until the end of the Lent term. In the lobbies and corridors of the main building, students were found sitting on floors, singing songs, 'holding endless discussions … reading, eating or just sleeping'.[17] Student-made banners were draped from the walls and slogans plastered across the blackboards that once neatly displayed official notices of school functions. Lectures and seminars had been cancelled due to low attendance, with up to 40% of the student body estimated to have been involved in the boycotts.[18] It was a peaceful takeover, a 'good-humoured affair', with some students reminiscing that it was a fun experience—perhaps even the highlight of their LSE years. The March occupation generated a unique sense of community among the 1966–1969 generation, an ephemeral feeling of camaraderie. The 'early revivalist' atmosphere of the era, as described by 1968 SU President Colin Crouch, is fondly remembered by those who were actively engaged in student activism.[19] Interestingly, although the occupation of 1967 created rifts between academics and students at the time, it fostered a sense of collective identity among students and forged vivid memories that some alumni still hold.[20] By the beginning of the summer

---

[15] *The Beaver*, 3 November 1966, p. 1.
[16] Dahrendorf 1995: 455.
[17] Ibid.
[18] Donnelly 2019b.
[19] LSE 2019.
[20] Wain & Sturdy 2015.

term, the Court of Governors had granted clemency to Adelstein and Bloom, suspending their penalties, and the occupation was adjourned.

By 1969, however, unrest on the LSE campus had taken a more sombre turn. As the protests continued, students were fervently and vehemently campaigning on a number of different issues. Energetic campaigns were held against the atrocities in Rhodesia and South Africa in 1968, and students were prominent in the anti-Vietnam War demonstration outside the US embassy in March 1968[21]—a protest that required 1,000 London policemen to be on crowd control duty. What became perhaps 'the unhappiest in the history of the School' began two weeks before the beginning of Michaelmas term of 1968.[22] The School authorities had begun installing security gates around the campus to protect the school buildings in the event of another, and more violent, sit-in. Collective paranoia grew and the gates became the symbol of oppression in the eyes of the student radicals. On 17 January 1969, the Students' Union passed an emergency motion demanding that the gates be removed. On 24 January, a jostling, clamorous mob of students stormed out of the SU meeting and started dismantling the gates with crowbars, pickaxes and sledgehammers. Over 100 policemen were called in by the School authorities and 30 students were arrested for criminal damage. The School closed and remained closed for another 25 days between January and February 1969. As Professor George Jones recalls, 'it was a very unpleasant time',[23] one that left a legacy of distrust and suspicion between staff and students, and which had deep implications for the dynamic between staff and students in the Government Department and the wider School community.

Students versus Staff

The student protests resulted in clear divisions on the School campus, manifesting primarily in two forms: internal clashes between academics *within* departments, and discord between faculty and students. In the Government Department, the main source of division was between students and staff. In a podcast entitled 'Red Flag over Houghton Street?', Professor Michael Cox affirmed: 'most of the staff were not on the radical students' side' during protests of the late 1960s.[24] This was true—the views and beliefs held by academics, particularly within the Government Department, were generally not reflective of those held by the radical students. The academics who *did* display public support of the protests were chastised, with some having their contracts terminated for encouraging protesters during the demolition of the gates in the Old Building

---

[21]   Donnelly 2019a.
[22]   Dahrendorf 1995: 460.
[23]   Jones & Cook 2015.
[24]   Cox 2019.

(albeit none from the Government Department).[25] Some of the academics remained neutral during the rebellion, wanting a quiet life with minimal disturbances to carry on with their teaching and research.[26] Others were strident opponents of the demonstrations. The late Professor George Jones, a member of the latter camp, narrated the occurrences at the School and the reactions within the Department at the time. Having joined the Department in 1966, Jones recalled how he and Professor Imre Lakatos—who had been trained by the KGB and was active in the Communist Party in Hungary prior to joining the LSE—had drawn up lists of those who were on their side, and those who were against. As Jones remarked, the protests 'poisoned relations and people remembered for many years afterwards who was on which side'.[27]

The majority of academics in the Government Department were staunch opponents of the student protests. Professor George Jones remarked that nearly all of his colleagues disapproved of the use of direct action and protest by students—unlike in other departments, most notably Sociology and Law, where a higher number of faculty endorsed the student demonstrations.[28] He attributed this to the fact that, as political scholars, the Government Department believed that 'you should conduct public affairs rationally'. There was consensus among the faculty that instead of protests and violence, students 'should work through representations and have reasoned argument'.[29] There was one individual in the Department, however, who did not share this viewpoint: Ralph Miliband. By demonstrating his support for the student protestors, the Marxist professor quickly became the lone wolf of the Department, and by the early 1970s, Miliband felt so alienated that he decided to leave the School.[30] Jones went so far as to declare that Miliband had been 'encourag[ing] disorder'[31] by supporting the student zealots. Emeritus Professor John Charvet recalls how the protests left Miliband feeling estranged: 'Miliband wouldn't speak to us after [the student protests], and he certainly wouldn't speak to me because I made a speech [in opposition of the student protestors]. He then left the school. It was a tense time.'[32]

Oakeshott, a man who habitually chose to remain uninvolved in the politics of the university, became unable to refrain from involving himself during the discontents of 1968. He was unconvinced by the character of the rebellions, believing the student protesters to have 'no genuine grievances', and going on to say that 'when you are dealing with thugs [staff and students], you must

---

[25] Ibid.
[26] Jones & Cook 2015.
[27] Ibid.
[28] Ibid.
[29] Ibid.
[30] Ibid
[31] Ibid.
[32] Charvet interview 2020.

shoot first', perfectly encapsulating the attitude among the upper echelons of the Department in response to the student demands. In a letter to the then-Director, he wrote:

> There are a small number of English boys and girls who regard university life as an opportunity to impose what they think as their political opinions upon captive audiences. They are highly organised and completely intolerant, and are dedicated to the destruction of 'bourgeois society', and regard universities as the soft underbelly vulnerable and defenceless.[33]

Oakeshott saw in the protestors a streak of revolutionary practice that would never be satisfied, regarding them as a destructive force, and believing School authorities and staff had the duty to put an end to the student delinquency. This belief was shared among those in his inner circle, including Professor Ken Minogue. In an article published in *The Beaver* on 1 February 1968, Minogue—Senior Lecturer in Political Science at the time—responded to a student who had written a piece demanding greater student involvement in the government of the School, published in the preceding issue. Explaining why power and administrative authority should not be proportionally distributed among students and staff, he argued that 'government of the School and the style of student politics don't get along very well together'.[34] In his view, the university should never be governed in the style of student politics—a style which he described as 'convulsive twitches' in response to 'enthusiastic inexperience'.[35] He wrote:

> LSE politics appear mainly to consist of faction meetings in smoky rooms, and dashing postures on the stage to the Old Theatre ... Might be good for cheer in the Union. But try and marry these two styles and there will be endless walkouts, accusations of bad faith, and all the petulance of those who are not getting what they want.[36]

In the same article, he described himself as one of many 'Political Apathetics'— those who do not wish to spend their life in politics and prefer to 'limit the application of democracy in institutional life'. Minogue stated 'Our beliefs arise, not from the lifeless pallor suggested by our enemies but because we have better things to do than deploy ourselves for the pseudo-excitements of the mass meeting'.[37] Minogue was one of several in the Department who held

---

[33] Oakeshott 1969.
[34] *The Beaver*, 1 February 1968, p. 3.
[35] Ibid.
[36] Ibid.
[37] Ibid.

Figure 14: Professor Kenneth Minogue, Circa 1980; Credit: LSE Library.

this viewpoint. In the eyes of the faculty, the student protests were futile and juvenile. Moreover, Minogue proceeded to draw parallels to the 'Laski Legend' in his response to the student: 'As I say, I found this passage puzzling in many ways, and wondered if I could not detect here the echo of the Laski Legend— one of those devices by which we flatter the dead in order to denigrate the living.'[38] What was already becoming clear by the early 1960s became even more apparent during the protests of 1966 to 1969: the Laski ethos was most certainly of a bygone era in the Government Department. His spirit, however, had been replaced by that of Oakeshott and his coterie of 'political apathetics' who vociferously opposed student rebellion.

While the LSE student protesters might have had their critics within the Government Department, they received praise from New Left activists at the time, such as Gareth Stedman Jones, Anthony Barnett and Tom Wengraf,[39] for engaging students in a novel way. As Troschitz notes, it was the 'first time students had shown unprecedented collective solidarity in their role as students'.[40] This common student identity, characterised by a shared propensity for direct action in the name of democracy, was central to the protests. Although students shifted their focus onto a number of different issues over the years—from the Adams affair, to the American involvement in Vietnam, to the imposition of the gates in the Old Building—the protesters were united by shared values and a common mode of expression.[41] The protests were thus the expression of a

[38] Ibid.
[39] Troschitz 2017: 106.
[40] Ibid.
[41] Ibid.

collective student identity, but also a means of fostering it. However, to say that the protests led to the emergence of a common LSE student identity for the first time would not be entirely accurate. A common student consciousness had already existed for decades,[42] but by the 1960s, this collective student identity had transmuted and taken an entirely new form: one that saw the administration as the enemy. The protests had revealed power imbalances within the School and within the Department, and differences in outlook and principles between faculty and students had become the major dividing factor on the LSE campus.

The student protests of the late 1960s also had a significant effect in shaping the reputation of the LSE as a radical and socialist-leaning institution. However, the popular image of the Department as a bastion of radical and socialist thought might have held little truth to it. When Ralph Miliband decided to leave the Department for Leeds in the early 1970s, Cox notes that the Department was in 'no hurry to replace him with someone of similar theoretical disposition or—I might add—of equal intellectual stature'.[43] Professor Tony Travers remarked that the LSE is often perceived from the outside as a 'sort of left-wing institution' and that this perception is particularly a result of what transpired in the 1960s.[44] Matt Matravers, an alumnus of the Department and Professor of Law at the University of York, echoes this sentiment: 'The reputation of the LSE had been far-left because of 1968, but I don't think LSE was actually right-wing or left-wing. It was even then a massively international, pluralistic place.' Matravers reflects that despite the external perception of the LSE and its political thinkers as 'radical socialists', the Government Department housed a number of figures from different ends of the political spectrum at the time and its syllabus was in fact 'pluralistic' and somewhat 'international'—at least, relative to other Political Science departments in the United Kingdom at the time.[45]

The Government Department did in fact host a multitude of scholars across the political spectrum, and the popular perception that the LSE was a hotbed of radical, socialist thought remained an exaggerated reputation. Conservative theorists such as Oakeshott, Minogue and Kedourie remained influential figures in the Department throughout the decade, mainly in charge of teaching political theory.[46] On the other side of the spectrum was George Jones, described as a 'kind of classic Wilsonian Fabian Labour' by his colleague Paul Kelly.[47] Finding themselves somewhere in the middle were academics such as Robert Orr, Ernest Thorp and John Charvet, all of whom would remain on the

---

[42] Ibid.
[43] Cox 2019.
[44] Travers interview 2020.
[45] Matravers interview 2020.
[46] LSE 1962: 421–436.
[47] Kelly interview 2020.

faculty until the early 1990s.[48] H. R. G. Greaves, who had lectured undergraduates in 'Contemporary Political Thought' and the British constitution since joining the School in 1930, included a wide range of thinkers on his syllabus: Bentham, Marx, Hegel, J. S. Mill, Lenin, Schumpeter and Wallas (and other Fabian texts).[49] Leonard Schapiro, who took up his three-year term as Convener from H. R. G. Greaves in 1969, taught modules on the Soviet Government, while Keith Panter-Brick tailored his research focus primarily towards civil war and decolonisation in Africa.[50] While the more radical emphasis Laski had once placed on the Department had long since disappeared, it remained a pluralistic centre for a range of political studies.

While the protests of the late 1960s created a tense time for the Department, they also resulted in some positive changes. First, Professor George Jones recalls how the troubles formed friendships and alliances across departments. It brought together staff members, who previously did not have much contact, but were united in the fight against the student rebels: 'because of the [protests] we got to know each other across departments ... I think it was really good for the cohesion of the School.'[51] The protests also prompted the Department and the School authorities to improve student–staff relations by increasing communication and feedback channels, such as frequent meetings between students and staff, and greater representation of students on School committees. Although the initial student demands were not met, and Sir Walter Adams did in fact take up the position of LSE Director in 1967—a position he retained until 1974—the protests permanently changed the dynamic between students and staff. A new era for the Department had begun, one where students were to become more active players in shaping its course.

Post-Oakeshottian Divide: Two Visions in Conflict

Alongside the changes which took place at the School in the early 1970s, one event was of particular significance for the Government Department—the retirement of Michael Oakeshott in 1968. Although he continued to attend various social and departmental meetings until his death in 1990, his departure marked the end of an era, and signalled an uncertain period for the future of the Department as an institution. As seen in Chapter 2, Oakeshott was a strong and charismatic figure with distinctive views, who not only managed to establish himself as one of the leading conservative political theorists and British public intellectuals while at the LSE, but also to attract quite a few disciples in the Department. After he stepped down, these scholars formed a group

---

[48] Travers interview 2020.

[49] LSE 1962: 429.

[50] Ibid.: 426.

[51] Cox 2019.

of political philosophers and historians with a shared intellectual identity and similar academic interests, but perhaps foremost a scepticism towards modern political science.

Oakeshott was the driving persona of the Department by the mid-1960s. Charvet recalls him to have been 'the dominant figure' at that time, with 'distinctive and actually very original views' that 'very much influenced the way he'd run the Department'.[52] His strong position was not only the result of his distinctive character, but also reflected some structural features. His long tenure as Convenor of the Department occurred before regulations were in place that limited the position to a three-year term, allowing him to exercise significant authority compared to his successors. The first of these, Professor Harold R. G. Greaves, took up the position in 1966, although Oakeshott would remain the informal head until he retired.

Although Oakeshott's retirement marked a historic moment, with the Department losing its guiding beacon, it was not the end of the Oakeshottian story in the Department. One of his lasting contributions was that he created several prominent academics in his own image; scholars trained by him, committed to the continuation and preservation of his way of thinking. Quite naturally, they became the Department's leading figures in the 1970s and 1980s. These individuals inherited a deep scepticism from Oakeshott towards modern political science, which was at the time already popular in the United States, but still relatively new in the United Kingdom. They considered political science to be a profound misconception of how one should analyse political life and human nature, arguing that the study of politics should consist of a historical investigation into the essence of human association with a particular focus on the well-established political and philosophical traditions.

As a result, in the early 1970s, the existing ideological divisions within the faculty had deepened. The Department had lost its natural and long-standing leader. Without Oakeshott, the split between academics trained or at least inspired by him and the rest of the faculty, particularly scholars in public administration and public policy, became apparent. Perhaps the most prominent of the so-called 'Oakeshottians' was Kenneth Minogue, unkindly called by his departmental colleague Bernard Crick 'Oakeshott's parrot'.[53] Within this circle were theorists and historians appointed in the 1950s and later, figures like Maurice Cranston, Leonard Schapiro and Elie Kedourie—all of them academics of an ideological orientation very much resembling that of Oakeshott.

Considering the Oakeshottians during the 1970s and 1980s, one cannot omit two distinctive men, Ernest Thorp and Robert Orr. Both were experienced lecturers, brought at a young age to the Department by Oakeshott in the 1960s, but both were, as we would now call it, 'research-inactive'. They rarely published, but appeared to be brilliant in 'transmitting the history of political

---

[52] Charvet interview 2020.
[53] O'Leary interview 2020.

thought from Oakeshott to the unwashed who appeared in front of him from time to time', particularly Ernest Thorp.[54] Brendan O'Leary mentions that Thorp 'rarely changed his notes and was always scrupulously accurate about the history of political thought'.[55] That accuracy was certainly useful for the role he had within the Department. Having an immense knowledge of the university regulations, he was a brilliant exams officer. Apart from that, starting in 1972, he sat on the School's Admissions Committee, managing undergraduate admissions at the Department.[56] He continued to be a member of this body throughout the 1970s, 1980s and 1990s, when he was also appointed Departmental Tutor.[57] The story of his appointment serves as a perfect example of how differently universities were run half a century ago. After completing his undergraduate degree at the LSE, Thorp worked for a bank. One day, Michael Oakeshott came into that same bank and appeared to offer him the position of a lecturer. After a short and inconclusive conversation over lunch, the young Thorp was convinced his candidacy had been rescinded. Yet, a couple of months later, he received a short letter from the LSE bursar with the key to the staff lavatory. This was how Thorp discovered that he had been appointed and was emblematic of the Government Department hiring procedures in place at the time.[58]

Among figures personally related to Oakeshott, there was also William Letwin. He was appointed in 1966, concentrating his academic work on economic theory and the history of economic thought, with a particular focus on the United States. Apart from being a lecturer and a scholar, he was also a central figure in the liberal intellectual salon in Kent Terrace, Regent's Park, visited by, among others, Isaiah Berlin, Friedrich Hayek and Oakeshott himself.[59] Letwin sustained it with his wife, Shirley. The couple played an important role in London political and cultural life and also in the Conservative renewal associated with Margaret Thatcher.[60] Shirley, being an academic herself and a close friend of Michael Oakeshott (who had devoted his central work, *On Human Conduct*, to 'S. R. L.', Shirley Robin Letwin), helped in a sense introduce many of the Oakeshottians, like Kenneth Minogue, to the prominent members of the political society. She also served as the Director for the Centre of Policy Studies, and though her role in hosting and shaping the conservative intellectual community of London was largely informal, it is hard to overlook the indirect impact the Letwins had on the Government Department and people associated with it around that time. Both were also influential in the operations of the

---

[54] Ibid.
[55] Ibid.
[56] LSE 1972: 47.
[57] *LSE Calendars*, from 1972–73 to 1989–90, LSE 1995.
[58] Matravers interview 2020.
[59] *The Telegraph* 2013.
[60] Minogue 1993.

Bruges Group, a think tank which advocated against British membership of the European Union.

On the other side of the divide within the Department were those we might describe as the 'non-Oakeshottians'. These were scholars like George Jones, an acclaimed figure in public administration and a recognised expert in local government. Along with William A. Robson, Jones was one of the founders of the Greater London Group, a research centre at the LSE that played a crucial role in the establishment of the Greater London Council in 1965. As Tony Travers, now professor at the Government Department and a former close colleague of George Jones, recalls, his work represented the tradition of the LSE from the activity of Sidney Webb and his engagement in the governance of London.[61] In cooperation with Bernard Donoughue, Jones wrote a biography of 'their gorgeous great hero',[62] Herbert Morrison, a Labour member of the war cabinet and a power behind the London Labour Party. Besides George Jones, strong figures in the public administration wing of the Department were accomplished academics like Peter Self, who would remain an influential member of the Greater London Group until his retirement in 1982.

In the late 1970s and early 1980s, new ideas were brought into the Department with the arrival of figures like Patrick Dunleavy in 1979 and Brendan O'Leary in 1981, both young and with academic interests contrasting to those of the Oakeshottians. Dunleavy, who retired from the Department in 2020 and whose research has focused on public policy, government and rational choice theory, describes his appointment as causing 'a big dispute in the appointment committee between him [Peter Self] and an Oakeshottian person who didn't want anybody to do public policy at all, thought it should be anathematised'.[63] This dispute illustrates the practical implications of the divide. O'Leary, appointed initially for a position in public administration, later became the Convenor of the comparative politics group within the Department. As an expert on Northern Ireland, he also played an important role in shaping government policies. Later he would serve as the Convenor of the Department, from 1998 to 2001.

Divisions in the Department are even apparent in the courses taught during the 1970s and 1980s. Oakeshottians specialised in lectures and seminars in political theory, which constituted a large part of the undergraduate and graduate courses at that time. Among the undergraduate courses was 'Political Thought of Hegel and Marx', delivered by Elie Kedourie, 'Political Thought from Hobbes to Burke', delivered by Kenneth Minogue, 'French Political Thought', led by Maurice Cranston, and 'Modern Political Thought', taken by Ernest Thorp.[64] Graduate students could also attend, among others, Oakeshott's flagship 'History of Political Thought' course, which he ran himself

---

[61] Travers interview 2020.
[62] Ibid.
[63] Dunleavy interview 2019.
[64] LSE 1975: 373–375.

Figure 15: The LSE Department of Government in 1975; Credit: LSE Library.

alongside Kenneth Minogue, Elie Kedourie, Robert Orr and John Charvet.[65] Non-Oakeshottians were involved in lectures in 'Modern Politics and Government with Special Reference to Britain', an introductory course for first-year students, given by George Jones, Rodney Barker and Bernard Donoughue, as well as 'Administrative Behaviour and Organisation', led by Peter Self, and 'Aspects of Comparative Local Government', given by George Jones.[66] Later in the 1980s, seminars in 'Public Policy Analysis' and 'Public Policy Formulation' were given by Patrick Dunleavy, and a seminar in 'Public Administration' began being taken by Brendan O'Leary.[67]

The disagreement between the Oakeshottians and their opponents was more about the general approach to political enquiry, which was touched on in Chapter 2. Oakeshott 'packed the Department with historians',[68] perceiving the study of politics as an attempt to reach 'the rich historical text understanding of mature traditions',[69] while maintaining 'a scepticism about what it didn't

---

[65] Ibid.
[66] Ibid., pp. 376–379.
[67] LSE 1987: 488–489.
[68] Charvet interview 2020.
[69] Kelly interview 2020.

regard as mature traditions'.[70] Oakeshottians stood against the idea of trying to measure things and employ precision to make political studies as scientific as possible. They saw the essence of the study of politics to consist of addressing broader questions concerning human activity for which no quantitative evidence may be found. This was the foundation for the opposition to modern political science, which was at that time taking hold, particularly in the United States. They also remained sceptical of public administration and public policy, as practised within the Department, often with direct historical reference to the Fabian ideals. They regarded this approach as too engaged in the running of political affairs. In short, the split within the faculty was in a sense part of a broader discussion between two approaches to the study of politics, one more qualitative, the other more quantitative, which continues until today. The historical circumstances of the 1970s, however, made it particularly salient.

This brief outline reveals the split into two camps across the period—political theorists and public administration and policy scholars. While the Oakeshottians certainly held a strong influence, they began to be joined by other groups whose interests lay outside the traditional focus of the Department. Rather than dominating the research agenda as they had during the 1960s, they now formed a dense circle of distinctive scholars with a strong representation among the staff. John Charvet, initially affiliated with that group, speaks about the time he joined the Department in the 1960s, noting that 'naturally, as a political theorist, I was absorbed in to what became clear to me was really an Oakeshottian coterie: a little band of Oakeshottians'.[71] Paul Kelly, now Professor of Political Philosophy at the LSE, remarks that even when he arrived in 1995, 'most of the political theory faculty were Oakeshott-trained or Oakeshott-inspired. Oakeshott was very much respected.'[72] However, with new academics joining from the early 1970s, many of them pursuing studies in comparative politics or rational choice theory, the dividing line between the right-wing group of political theorists and the rest of the faculty became less discernible.

However, while several prominent professors continued to teach throughout the 1970s and early 1980s, the Government Department was not considered a leading centre of political research. It still bore the reputation gained during 1968 for socialist activism and political radicalism, which cast a long shadow on the reputation of the School. Rodney Barker, Emeritus Professor of Government in the Department, notes it was commonly believed that when he arrived at the LSE in 1971 it was 'a communist-dominated'[73] institution, despite the internal dominance of the Oakeshottians. In 1981, these opinions had shifted, with the *Wall Street Journal* critically writing that 'the school renowned as a Socialist breeding ground actually harbours what may be the most right-wing

---

[70] Ibid.
[71] Charvet interview 2020.
[72] Kelly interview 2020.
[73] Barker interview 2020.

department of government in the West'.[74] These contradictory opinions on the character of the Government Department during the period demonstrate its internal divisions well. It lacked a clear and dominant intellectual identity, let alone a focus for future research. Paul Kelly even notes that in the 1980s it was even considered 'a hotbed of mediocrity',[75] an institution that trained many good academics, but was living off its past glory. Part of the reason for this was that its leading academics, like Elie Kedourie and Kenneth Minogue, were at the end of their careers and close to retirement. Michael Oakeshott would still convene his 'History of Political Thought' seminar until 1981, and attended many events until his death in 1990, but he was no longer the driving force within the Department or the School as a whole.

Thatcherism and the Transformation of Academia

The 1970s and 1980s brought the collapse of the post-war consensus in Britain, marking the end of a shared belief of both Conservative and Labour Party in Keynesian economics, an expansive welfare state, strong trade unions and nationalisation. The deep recession of 1973 and the following years of economic stagnation forced governments around Europe to find savings in various sectors, including higher education. The beginning of the Thatcher government in 1979 amplified the existing trends towards free markets, deregulation and privatisation. Growth in numbers of student enrolments, deep cuts in higher education funding and the introduction of Research Assessment frameworks resulted in what is now referred to as the marketisation of academia. These wide-ranging changes in higher education in the United Kingdom altered the nature of the academic community and intellectual work itself. They also fundamentally changed the character of the LSE Government Department.

To better understand this period, one must take a closer look at the British higher education reforms in the early 1960s, particularly the Robbins Report of 1963. The recommendations of the government commission chaired by Lord Robbins, himself a prominent economist at the LSE, which met between 1961 and 1963 to discuss the problems of Britain's higher education, were simple— universities needed an immediate expansion to become more accessible and meet the challenges of the growing post-war economy. The Robbins Report in a sense only endorsed what was already happening. In 1961, the University of Sussex, the first of the eight planned new university campuses, later referred to as 'plate-glass universities' owing to their modern architectural design, was opened.[76] One year later, in 1962, fees were abolished in order to help students from poorer families obtain access to higher education. The number of

---

[74] Newman 1981.
[75] Kelly interview 2020.
[76] Anderson 2016.

university enrolments increased annually. Overall participation in higher education, measured as a proportion of students obtaining university degrees, rose from 3.4% in 1950, to 8.4% in 1970 and to 19.3% in 1990.[77] The 1972 Education White Paper, produced by Edward Heath's government and presented to Parliament by the then Secretary of State for Education and Science, Margaret Thatcher, entitled 'Education: Framework for Expansion', predicted that this trend would continue for at least the next 10 years.[78]

The growing number of students meant that the sum of teaching grants transferred to British universities each year by the University Grants Committee (UGC), a central body consisting mainly of academics deciding on where public money needed to be spent in higher education, had been steadily increasing over the 1970s, making universities almost entirely dependent on state funding.[79] The shock of 1973, caused by the OAPEC oil embargo targeted at nations supporting Israel in the Yom Kippur War, including the United Kingdom, resulted in drastic rises in global oil prices. The British Government had to find savings somewhere, and this in turn had a significant effect on the budgets of universities. In 1979, the newly formed Thatcher cabinet announced that the UGC would no longer pay the universities for foreign students, who would subsequently be charged with full fees,[80] an announcement that 'shook the very foundations of the School's funding structure'.[81] The reaction of the LSE, at which the proportion of overseas students accounted for 37% at that time,[82] was to limit spending per student, freeze new appointments and further increase the number of enrolments. Consequently, the School started to grow at an unprecedented rate. In the academic year 1967–1968, it had 3,439 regular students.[83] By 1984–1985, this number had reached 4,447.[84] Budgetary pressure on universities forced them to focus on increasing the number of students rather than teaching quality which, as Dahrendorf writes, had to result in 'a decline in standards'.[85]

In line with cost-saving measures, the Thatcher government also brought the beginning of what was to become known as the marketisation of higher education, with its new models of funding based on research and teaching excellence assessments. Cuts were often accompanied by a narrative which accused universities of being 'cartels of producers interest', which followed monopolistic practices

---

[77] National Committee of Inquiry into Higher Education 1997: Table. 1.1.
[78] Department of Education and Science 1972.
[79] Anderson 2016.
[80] Williams 1984: 265.
[81] Dahrendorf 1995: 497.
[82] Ibid.
[83] LSE 1967: 141.
[84] LSE 1985: 144.
[85] Dahrendorf 1995: 498.

without consideration to students and the taxpayers who funded them.[86] In 1985, as a pilot exercise, funding for research and teaching was separated within the UGC regime,[87] followed by the establishment of the Research Assessment Exercise in 1986, a peer-review-based research exercise scheme to define the research quality at each university. The next year, in a policy paper entitled 'Higher education: meeting the challenge', Thatcher's government mandated that universities should 'serve the economy more effectively and have closer links with industry and commerce, and promote enterprise'.[88] Following these recommendations, the 1988 Education Reform Act abolished the University Grants Committee regime, replacing traditional grants with 'contracts' which contained precise performance goals and indicators. Under the new policies, which were aimed at promoting a strong research culture and incentivise productivity, universities receiving poor assessment on research and those with numerous 'research inactive' scholars were to receive little or no funding, which meant that some of them would find themselves in a very difficult financial situation.[89]

These profound changes in the approach to higher education were met with serious criticism from the academic community, particularly among experienced scholars, who judged them to be an assault on the culture of academic freedom. Academics in the Government Department were at the centre of that discussion, particularly the representatives of the Oakeshottians for whom the proposed reforms were just another step in the continuing expansion of 'managerialism', an idea that ran counter to the very essence of academic activity. In his 1988 and 1989 essays entitled 'Diamonds into Glass: The Government and the Universities' and 'Perestroika in the Universities', Elie Kedourie strongly criticised the Research Assessment Exercise for increasing government control over universities, replacing accountability with factual management, and establishing arbitrary assessment criteria.[90] His essays not only criticised the government for wrongly seeking to quantify academic excellence while neglecting a whole spectrum of criteria that may not be expressed in numbers, but also for pursuing an irrational and destructive policy of increasing the number of enrolments while reducing the cost per student.[91]

To a large degree, Professor Kedourie's essays were a reaction to the broader transformation of the Department over the 1970s and 1980s, as it sought to adapt to the requirements of a new model of university education. This new model promoted egalitarianism and opening higher education to a broader mass of students. The process of turning 'diamonds into glass', as Kedourie puts it, meant that universities were to be run more like businesses in order to stay

---

[86] Kedourie 1993: 60.
[87] Anderson 2016.
[88] Department of Education and Science 1987.
[89] Barnard 1998.
[90] Kedourie 1993: 91–92.
[91] Ibid: 81.

in a good financial condition, 'producing' graduates and providing them with skills necessary in their further careers. The Oakeshottians were not the only scholars to notice that the Department was adapting to this new model. As George Jones, a prominent figure in the public administration group, mentions, the Department used to be a close community of scholars governing themselves and doing research, with students coming to learn from them. From the 1970s, this model was giving way to one founded on 'professional managerialism'.[92] The very structure of the School had changed, so that academics were perceived to be employees in a large educational corporation with limited participation in the governing bodies.

The location of the Department also in a sense reflected its different character prior to the transformation under the new policies. First, the Government Department was not located in one singular place, as it later came to be. Academics had their offices around the campus, although it is true that most of them resided in King's and Lincoln's Chambers. Paul Kelly mentions that the community would group around activities and that 'very important were the key seminars that used to bring students together or even faculty or both, because that was where you saw your colleagues ... That was where you got together.'[93] There was little need for office space for the administration personnel, since at that time these consisted of just a few secretaries. Small and quite shabby rooms in King's and Lincoln Chambers, filled with the smell of coffee and cigarettes, and with its steep and dangerous staircase, were hardly a suitable quarters for an efficient administration, yet this was the first home for a group of people with a shared passion for the study of politics. What is also significant is that for most courses at that time there was no distinction between lecturers and class teachers. Senior academics were engaged in teaching, having direct contact with students, which helped build a sense of a close community.

With the expansion of academia and growing cohorts of students, that model had become unsustainable. The Research Assessment Exercise (later the Research Excellence Framework) enforced a deeper academic specialisation and professionalisation. As Nicholas Barr remarks, 'even before the REF, departments were sort of increasingly becoming salient'.[94] Subject-specific assessment criteria further strengthened their role as independent and large entities, particularly from the late 1980s. As a result, the sense of community was partially replaced with more formal administrative structures. A more effective division of labour prevailed. Teaching became mostly the responsibility of junior staff, with senior academics concentrating on conducting research and writing publications to help the departments gain sufficient funding. This was a natural response to the new expectations towards higher education. It

---

[92] Jones & Cook 2015.
[93] Kelly interview 2020.
[94] Barr interview 2020.

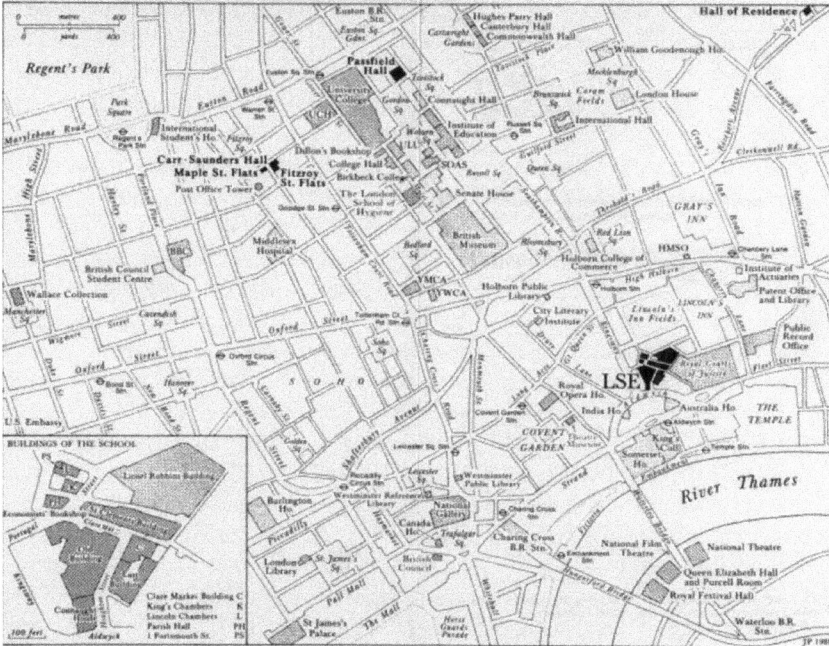

Figure 16: Map of the School, 1988–1989: Credit: LSE Library.

helped the Government Department emerge as a leading global centre of political science in the 1990s, but something precious was also irreversibly lost.

Conclusion

What had begun as a small-scale protest against the appointment of Sir Walter Adams soon escalated into perhaps the greatest turmoil in the history of the LSE. Events of the late 1960s not only affected the School's reputation, but revealed deep political divisions between academics, who expressed support for the protesters and those who adamantly opposed their activity. Scholars at the Government Department, dominated by mostly conservative thinkers like Oakeshott, in majority stood against the student revolt. The memory of the 'dense' atmosphere of that time, which encouraged Ralph Miliband to leave the School, prevailed throughout the 1970s. Protests had proven to be a great test for the unity of the Department. They also served as an impulse to democratise relations between staff and students.

Intellectual divisions remained the hallmark of the next two decades following Michael Oakeshott's retirement. The Department had many distinctive academics, but lacked a clear identity and, as a result, found itself divided between two different approaches to political science. With time, these divisions started to disappear, but there was a strong feeling during the 1970s and 1980s that the Department was living on its past glory. It was filled with distinctive personalities but ceased to be a leading research centre. With new scholars joining and bringing new approaches, these dynamics began to change, but this was also the product of external factors. In 1979, the Thatcher government started to reform British academia and the Government Department became a part of that process. The policies of the 1980s helped initiate the developments that eventually transformed the Department into a leading global centre of political science. However, this was only to take shape a decade later under the convenorship of Brian Barry.

These cross-currents left the venerable Department of Government in a state of uncertainty as the 20th century entered its final decade. By now, it had reached maturity, yet the influential figures that had shaped its rise had begun to disappear from its ranks, and internal disagreements over political and philosophical matters placed great strain on those who now took charge. The older band of Oakeshottians still dominated its image and agenda, yet their influence was to rapidly diminish over the coming decade. A quiet revolution had begun on the public policy side of the Department, building up a new body of expertise in analytical and research-heavy matters which fundamentally conflicted with the Oakeshottian vision of a liberal education. As the 1980s rolled over into the 1990s, these voices began making themselves heard, setting the stage for a rejuvenation of the Department's image at the turn of the millennium.

References

Anderson, R 2016 University fees in historical perspective. *History & Policy*, 8 February, http://www.historyandpolicy.org/policy-papers/papers/university-fees-in-historical-perspective.

Barnard, J W 1998 Reflections on Britain's research assessment exercise. *Journal of Legal Education*, 48(4), December: 467–495.

Cox, M 2019 Red flag over Houghton Street? The radical tradition at LSE—myth, reality, fact. *LSE History: Telling the Story of LSE* (audio blog), 16 January, https://blogs.lse.ac.uk/lsehistory/2019/01/16/red-flag-over-houghton-street-the-radical-tradition-at-lse-myth-reality-fact/.

Crouzet, F 1969 A university besieged: Nanterre, 1967–69. *Political Science Quarterly*, 84(2): 328–350. DOI: https://doi.org/10.2307/2147263.

Dahrendorf, R 1995 *LSE: A history of the London School of Economics and Political Science 1895–1995*. Oxford: Oxford University Press.

Department of Education and Science 1972 *Education: A framework for expansion*. Cmnd. 5174, London (December).

Department of Education and Science 1987 *Higher education: Meeting the challenge*. Cm 114, London (April).

Donnelly, S 2019a 'Adams closed it, we opened it'—student occupation in October 1968. *LSE History: Telling the Story of LSE* (blog), 25 February, https://blogs.lse.ac.uk/lsehistory/2019/02/25/adams-closed-it-we-opened-it-student-occupation-in-october-1968/.

Donnelly, S 2019b 'Opposing a director', *LSE History: Telling the Story of LSE* (blog), 18 February, https://blogs.lse.ac.uk/lsehistory/2019/02/18/the-lse-troubles-opposing-a-director/.

Jones, G and **Cook, C** 2015 Tales from Houghton Street: George Jones. Interview, 22 July, LSE Digital Library, https://digital.library.lse.ac.uk/objects/lse:kub826huw.

Kedourie, E 1993 The British universities under duress: Two essays by Professor Elie Kedourie. *Minerva*, 31(1): 56–75.

LSE 1962 *The London School of Economics and Political Science, University of London, Calendar for the sixty-eighth session, 1962–1963*. London: London School of Economics and Political Science.

LSE 1967 *The London School of Economics and Political Science, University of London, Calendar for the seventy-third session, 1967–1968*. London: London School of Economics and Political Science.

LSE 1972 *The London School of Economics and Political Science, University of London, Calendar for the seventy-eighth session, 1972–1973*. London: London School of Economics and Political Science.

LSE 1975 *The London School of Economics and Political Science, University of London, Calendar for the eighty-first session, 1975–76*. London: London School of Economics and Political Science.

LSE 1985 *The London School of Economics and Political Science, University of London, Calendar for the ninety-first session, 1985–86*. London: London School of Economics and Political Science.

LSE 1987 *The London School of Economics and Political Science, University of London, Calendar for the ninety-third session, 1987–88*. London: London School of Economics and Political Science.

LSE 1995 *The London School of Economics and Political Science, University of London, Calendar for the one hundred and first session, 1995–1996*. London: London School of Economics and Political Science.

LSE 2019 The LSE protests 1966–69, 16 September, online video, 14:40, https://www.youtube.com/watch?v=dQ3ZxqZRDhU.

London School of Economics Students, *LSE's New Director: A Report on Walter Adams* (London: Agitator Pamphlet, 1966), 18.

Minogue, K 1993 Obituary: Shirley Letwin (1924–93). *Political Studies*, 41(4): 683–684.

National Committee of Inquiry into Higher Education 1997 *Report 6 Widening participation in higher education for students from lower socio-economic groups and students with disabilities* (Dearing Report).

Newman, B 1981 Academic paradox: Famed British college has a Leftist label it doesn't deserve, *Wall Street Journal*, 29 July.

No author 1967 Dr. Adams and the London School of Economics. *Minerva*, 5(2): 312–315, http://www.jstor.org/stable/41822701.

Oakeshott, M 1969 *Letter to the director*, 26 January. British Library of Political and Economic Sciences.

The Telegraph 2013 Professor William Letwin, Obituary, 4 March.

Troschitz, R 2017 *Higher education and the student: From welfare state to neo-liberalism*. London: Routledge Taylor & Francis Group.

Wain, C and **Sturdy, T** 2015 Tales from Houghton Street: Carol Wain (Hornsey), interview, 10 July, https://digital.library.lse.ac.uk/objects/lse:ceq683nov.

Williams, P 1984 Britain's full-cost policy for overseas students. *Comparative Education Review*, 28(2), May: 258–278.

Interviews

Barker, Rodney, interview by Hilke Gudel, 10 February 2020.

Barr, Nicholas, interview by Hilke Gudel, 16 April 2020.

Charvet, John, interview by Sara Luxmoore, 18 February 2020.

Dunleavy, Patrick, interview by Cheryl Schonhardt-Bailey, 6 December 2019.

Headland, Jane, interview by Hilke Gudel, 20 February 2020.

Kelly, Paul, interview by Lukasz Kremky, 13 February 2020.

Matravers, Matt, interview by Hilke Gudel, 22 May 2020.

O'Leary, Brendan, interview by Hilke Gudel, 3 February 2020.

Travers, Tony, interview by Hilke Gudel, 25 March 2020.

CHAPTER 4

New Dawn

The Turn of the Millennium, 1990–2020

Daniel Skeffington, Hilke Gudel and Sara Luxmoore

Introduction

The 1990s marked a period of significant change for higher education institutions in the United Kingdom, with reforms conducted throughout the 1980s
laying the groundwork for a further professionalisation of academic life. These
organisational and cultural transformations were accompanied by a change in
demographics, with more and more women entering higher education, both as
students but also as professors, and the overall student body growing increasingly international. The School also began a wider pivot of its student body
towards the European Union, opening up the Government Department to an
influx of new students from all over the continent. As the Thatcher era drew to
a close on 28 November 1990, these changes were beginning apace.

From the historical perspective of the Government Department, however,
these professional reforms coincided with another, more symbolic event. Three
weeks later, on 18 December, Michael Oakeshott passed away at his home in
Acton,[1] marking the end to an era that dominated the study of political science

---

[1] Franco & Marsh 2012: 1.

How to cite this book chapter:
Skeffington, D., Gudel, H. and Luxmoore, S. 2021. New Dawn: The Turn of the
Millennium, 1990–2020. In: Schonhardt-Bailey, C. and Bannerman, G. (eds.) *Political Science at the LSE: A History of the Department of Government, from the Webbs
to COVID.* Pp. 111–135. London: Ubiquity Press. DOI: https://doi.org/10.5334
/bcn.e. License: CC-BY-NC

at the School since the early 1950s. And, while the Oakeshottians did continue to hold appointments in the Department, they grew less influential with each passing year. Elie Kedourie and Maurice Cranston each stayed on throughout the 1990–1991 academic year, teaching on 'The Political Thought of Hegel and Marx' and 'The History of Political Thought'. Ken Minogue remained on the faculty until his retirement in 1995, and Ernest Thorp until 2003. However, their prior standing in the Department was much diminished, and a new empirical orthodoxy had become the focus of a reinvigorated and research-oriented Department of Government, as John Major stepped into Downing Street.

A Different Way of Thinking: Brian Barry

This effort of professionalisation was led by Brian Barry, perhaps the last of the Department's great 'eccentrics' who had been so prevalent in previous decades. Barry arrived at the LSE in 1987 from the California Institute of Technology, having held previous positions at Birmingham, Keele, Oxford, Essex, British Columbia and Chicago. He took a First in Philosophy, Politics and Economics at Queen's College, Oxford, spending a year at Harvard with John Rawls before earning his DPhil. under the supervision of the famous analytic legal philosopher, H. L. A. Hart, in 1964.[2] Barry, who by the time of his appointment had become a leading analytic philosopher in his own right, was a committed empirical social scientist. And, while he would remain at the School for just 11 years, his influence on the character of the Department was profound.

Barry was an interesting personality, even in a Department characterised by a run of esoteric and maverick leaders. He convened a meeting of rational choice theorists and other 'positive' political scientists at his Bloomsbury flat, colloquially known as 'The Rationals', many of whom would go on to play major roles in the future of the Department.[3] Professor Kai Spiekermann recalls that once, during the weekly Thursday gathering of the political theorists at the LSE Beaver's Retreat, he and Barry got into a heated argument over the 20 July 'Operation Valkyrie' plot to assassinate Hitler, masterminded by the German Army Colonel Claus von Stauffenberg. Barry loudly exclaimed that von Stauffenberg was a 'coward' and should have remained in the room to kill Hitler, rather than leaving the briefcase unattended to explode, which ultimately caused the plot to fail.[4] Barry also struggled with bipolar disorder throughout his life, a condition which affected his relationship with students and staff at times. He could be short with pupils, and sometimes difficult. Brian 'didn't tolerate much

---

[2] Kelly 2009.
[3] Kelly interview 2020.
[4] Kai Spiekermann, personal communication, 2020.

Figure 17: Professor Brian Barry in 2004, celebrating July 4th at a barbeque
hosted by Professor Cheryl Schonhardt-Bailey.

nonsense', and his 'very high intellectual standards'—which were such a blessing
for his academic work—led to tension with others on occasion, recalls Albert
Weale, a former doctoral student of Barry's and Emeritus Professor of Political Theory and Public Policy.[5] On at least one occasion, there were accounts
of PhD students who left due to his somewhat volatile personality. However,
despite these frictions, Barry is always recalled with great affection and generosity by those who knew him personally. He was another larger-than-life personality in a Department characterised by similar titans of political thought
who were enthusiastic, difficult and brilliant.

Barry's intellectual legacy remains widely recognised even today. His doctoral thesis, published in 1965 as 'Political Argument', came to be 'one of the
principal contributions to the development of post-war political theory', and
'remains a compendium of how we conceptualize, analyse and defend claims
about democracy, power and justice'.[6] His writings on political philosophy
were recognised through elections to major fellowships during his career,
joining the British Academy in 1988 and later the American Academy of Arts
and Sciences. He was also the only British academic to receive the prestigious

---

[5] Weale telephone interview 2020.
[6] Ibid.

Johann Skytte prize from the University of Uppsala, a recognition for his contributions to the study of political science.

However, Barry's lasting legacy at the School went beyond pure scholarship. Although he was Convenor for only two years, from 1993 to 1995, the institutional reforms he implemented in the Government Department had a strong impact on the scholarship that was to follow. 'He was a great institution-builder' and a 'very good talent spotter': he 'could fit people to jobs very well' and 'get them working for the common good'.[7] He had also arrived at a time when an important group of emerging political scientists were beginning to make their mark on the Department's character. Rodney Barker, Patrick Dunleavy and George Jones taught key courses on the BSc, such as 'Modern Politics and Government, with Special Reference to Britain'.[8] Jones had previously been Convenor of the Department in the mid-1980s and Barker would go on to hold the Convenership of the Department from 2007 to 2009. Dunleavy would feature heavily in the empirical restructuring plan long after Barry and his successor, Christopher Hood, had departed. All three helped build this new vision for the Department, focused on rigour, research and a global reputation.

The importance of the institutional reforms Barry implemented is hard to overstate, and to fully appreciate their significance requires revisiting the historical context. Barry was 'basically told to sort out the Department' as it 'was a failing Department'.[9] As seen in Chapter 2, the appointments process during the 1950s and 1960s was informal and ad hoc. Appointments were conducted through personal networks, often through Oakeshott himself, driven by a unified idea of what the Department stood for and the sort of faculty that would help realise that. The idea of a competitive process for professional recruitment was not prevalent at the time. As Brendan O'Leary recalls, for one new lectureship:

> Oakeshott goes to Dublin and he hears a lecture on medieval political thought by John Morrell. He has a drink at the bar with Morrell at the University College Dublin, and he says to Morrell: Please, show up to LSE on Monday, I have a job for you. Morrell and his wife had a real row because his wife could not believe he was going to be offered a job by Oakeshott in this manner. Morrell decided to take the risk and flew to London. He arrived and Oakeshott gave him a job, a lectureship in political theory. At Morrell's departure speech, he said that he was given no employment contract, he was given no guidance to his actual duties, he got the rough idea that maybe he had to show up twice a week to perform his teaching duties and that was it.[10]

---

[7] Ibid.
[8] LSE 1990.
[9] Dowding interview 2020.
[10] O'Leary interview 2020.

This lack of a competitive recruitment process also meant that academics were under far less pressure to publish frequently. Professor Matt Matravers, who studied at the School from 1987 to 1994, recalls that for some LSE academics publishing was not a great priority.[11] In fact, some, such as the Oakeshottian scholar Ernest Thorp, had hardly published anything during their time.

In Barry's eyes, scholars who did not publish were 'creatures from another age'.[12] To refocus and reformulate the Department, he arranged to have dinners with those he felt he could persuade to leave, trying to convince them that it was in their interest to retire early.[13] He found many were quite happy to take early retirement, realising that they had not found their careers in academia particularly fulfilling. In a similar vein, Barry conducted an audit of all the rooms under his control, and discovered that the famous philosopher Sir Karl Popper still had a secretary who was receiving his mail for him. As Popper had retired in 1969 and died in 1994, the secretary was redundant, and she was asked to leave her post.

The need to publish and to receive research grants had been impressed upon him throughout his career in the United States, which to some members of staff was 'a bit of a shock'.[14] Key appointments such as Keith Dowding and Cheryl Schonhardt-Bailey were made during his tenure, appointments which influenced the character of the Department long after Barry had left. He began by taking over courses on 'Modern Political Philosophy: Justice', co-running the first-year course and the second-year seminar on 'Political Philosophy' with John Charvet and Robert Orr, alongside Maurice Cranston and Brendan O'Leary.[15] At the time—and up until 1995—the BSc (Econ.) remained the School's renowned 'first degree', integrating a number of subjects from political philosophy to applied economics under several 'streams'. The Convener of the Department during Barry's early years was Gordon Smith, who led third-year BSc courses on topics such as 'Comparative Political Analysis', as well as the politics and government of Eastern Europe and Germany.[16]

The transformation that took place at the faculty level also affected the doctoral training in the Department, which became much more formalised over the years. While the system provided good one-to-one supervision, it was not a rigorously structured programme with seminars or dedicated training. Competitive recruitment processes were virtually absent. In response, Barry reorganised the Department to emphasise these aspects. Initially, PhD students were not funded in the Department, which meant the School attracted applicants of a variable sort of academic quality and cohorts tended to be larger

[11] Matravers interview 2020.
[12] Ibid.
[13] Dowding interview 2020.
[14] Matravers interview 2020.
[15] LSE 1987: 488; LSE 1988: 485, 487.
[16] LSE 1989: 510–511.

in size. Funding and selectiveness have resulted in more rigorous methods training and an overall better preparation for the academic job market. Teaching responsibilities for undergraduate students were, to a large extent, also transferred to PhD students or Fellows and away from members of staff, thus allowing academics to focus on research rather than teaching class material to undergraduates.[17]

While Barry's leadership played a significant role in promoting professionalism in the LSE Government Department, there were also more long-term, structural trends that supported this change in direction. And, while they had influenced Barry's time as Convener, they were to form the central issue for his successors as the century neared its end.

A Changing Landscape

After a brief, year-long stint under the direction of Alan Beattie—during which he 'continued to work hard to adapt the Department ... to the modern British academic realities'[18]—Christopher Hood took on the Convenership in 1995, continuing to implement the turn towards professionalisation initiated by Brian Barry. He joined the LSE from the University of Sydney in 1989, where he had been Professor of Public Administration, and upon arriving assumed command over several new and emerging courses at the LSE. In addition to helping run the Department's MSc in Public Administration and Public Policy, he co-founded both the MSc in Regulation and the Centre for the Analysis of Risk and Regulation. Hood's first few days as Convener were perhaps not as smooth as he would have hoped, and he was beset by a series of issues. On his first day, he received a phone call telling him that Brian Barry had been seriously injured in a car accident. Shortly after this, several computers were stolen from the Department. Finally, there was a phone call from the Finance Department saying that there was a black hole of almost £100,000 in the Department's spending from the previous year that was unaccounted for, and that evidence needed to be provided about this potentially improper conduct. This atmosphere of rapid problem solving was to set the tone for the late 1990s.

One of the major issues confronting both Barry and Hood was the creeping shift of the LSE's business structure, following the commercialisation of higher education in universities across Britain since the 1980s. As we shall see in the section entitled 'New Blood', below, this move worked in tandem with a reorientation in the Department's focus and hiring strategy. Moving towards more of a business model in their management approach, universities now increasingly emphasised their marketing and branding towards potential applicants. The School shifted towards a one-year taught Masters' model, which

[17] Matravers interview 2020.
[18] Lieven 2001: xxiii.

subsequently meant an increase in the number of overseas fee-paying students. It was a certain kind of business model which had far-reaching implications for the composition of the student body of the Government Department. There were fewer traditional British and Commonwealth students, with more international students arriving from the European Union, America and China. Barry's reforms had built on a broad-based realignment of the Department's research agenda, reorienting its focus to Europe and America. The West German Group led by Gordon Smith was influential in driving this research focus from 1992 to 1997, while the European Institute was also founded in 1991, hosting a string of new collaborative appointments between the Institute and the Department. In 1992, the Department even founded a joint BA in European Studies with King's College London, a programme whose three streams, 'On Europe', 'On France' and 'On Germany', allowed for student specialisation.[19] Under Hood, this initial shift was reflected in the type of work being done by the Department, and the types of students and faculty it was attracting.

The most noticeable changes besides the outward recruitment drive for new students was the growing importance of research league tables and university rankings. Domestic rankings of British universities were first published in 1993 by *The Times Good University Guide* and have since become an influential factor in the university selection process by students. There are four main league tables at present: *The Times*, the *Sunday Times*, *The Guardian* and the *Complete University Guide*. Since 2008, *Times Higher Education* has compiled a 'Table of Tables', which summarises the results from the three main domestic rankings in any given year. The main objective of the league tables was to inform potential undergraduate applicants about UK universities—this is achieved through a range of criteria, including but not limited to entry standards, student satisfaction, staff/student ratio, academic services, research quality, completion rates and student destinations. They provide prospective students with relevant information on the quality of universities and degrees so that they can make informed choices. As such, the rise of university rankings is also an expression of the marketisation of the sector. All league tables also rank universities on their strength in individual subjects. Since their inception the Department has performed to a high standard of research, reflecting the efforts made to improve its standing in research assessments since the late 1980s.

This change paralleled efforts to bring the Department more in line with political science in the United States, altering the appointments structure for new faculty. The School moved its calendar in line with the US appointments system to increase the number of American applications. Previously, the appointments process involved inviting all candidates for a position to visit the School for one day, during which they would be interviewed, back-to-back, in the morning, and would (in some, but not all, cases) give presentations—again back-to-back—in the afternoon. Candidates were grilled by a panel of

[19] Hix interview 2020.

six academics from the School, two from the Government Department, and four from other departments, for just 20 minutes. This process was extended after the Americanised reforms were introduced, with each candidate allocated one full day during which the appointments panel could get to know them individually, while simultaneously aiming to promote the benefits of the Department to them. The intention behind the change was on the one hand to attract the best candidates globally, both by making appointments at the same time as US universities and giving each potential applicant sufficient time in the Department itself. Alongside this more professional intent, the other aim was to create a more equitable and fair appointments system, one that would ideally result in more female and minority candidate appointments.

Despite general agreement on the scope and substance of this new appointment procedure, this change was not without some hiccups. One of the main criticisms came from Anne Phillips, who argued the new process may work against the appointment of more female and minority candidates. The concern was that the day-long interview, involving an evening dinner, would advantage more privileged and male candidates due to the emphasis on how well they fit within the existing Departmental work group. On the other hand, Simon Hix and Paul Kelly supported the decision, saying that research has shown that female candidates do best when competing for positions, and this new process would increase competition by reducing the role of 'insular groups' in appointments. The goal was to attract the best candidates, rather than friends, and this was believed to be the best way to make the process more equitable. Phillips's concerns, though well grounded, were not borne out when this new selection process was implemented, and the number of female academics steadily increased in the following years.

Another central event during Hood's tenure was the Research Assessment Exercise (RAE), carried out in 1996. The RAE, now known as the Research Excellence Framework, was and remains a highly consequential development for universities, conducted to assess the quality of the research output of the institution, and to rank them accordingly. Hood presided over the first RAE where the Department had to select which members were to be entered for consideration. Previous assessments had seen the work of all eligible staff that submitted for assessment. As the RAE ranks universities based on the quality of their research profile, it became a 'highly contentious' event that had to be 'thought about very carefully'.[20] A judgment had to be made 'about what kind of research would give us the topmost grade', a vital boost to the reputation of the Department at the time, while not offending or upsetting those faculty who would not be selected. It was a difficult affair to negotiate, and although the Department eventually gained the top grade from the exercise, Hood recalls

---

[20] Hood, telephone interview 2020.

it as a time of intense pressure for the School's professional vision of political science. 'My head would have been on the block, if we had not.'[21]

The significance the Department began to place on the RAE marked a new effort to have research drive the agenda of the School. Previously, following Lord Lionel Robbins's famous report in 1963, universities had placed most of their emphasis on 'teaching students how to think' by allowing research to coexist with the learning process.[22] Teaching and research were the twin pillars of university education, the former dedicated to instructing undergraduates in the basic modes of thinking, and the latter the 'advancement and preservation of knowledge'.[23] Yet, policies adopted under the Thatcher government and its successors aimed to reorient this approach. An increase in managerial practices at the LSE coincided with this tilt towards research; 'a move towards departmental administrators, who were serious managers and paid serious money'.[24] The first of these was hired under Alan Beattie, followed by Christopher Hood's appointment of Nicole Boyce, who remained manager of the Department for almost 20 years. At that time, the Department also started taking a more inclusive approach to managing its affairs, involving graduate-level students in the running of the Department. These changes marked a Department increasingly conscious of both its internal management structure and of the job prospects of its students—one where research had become the dominant mode of practice.

However, this trend towards professionalisation in higher education has not always been seen as a positive phenomenon. While the Department's productivity and calibre of research has increased, many also lament a certain spirit having been lost along the way. Academics are under pressure to publish high-quality articles frequently, leading some scholars to suggest a one-article-per-year limit to curb this excessive demand.[25] Moreover, the traditional view of the university as a group of scholars, researchers and students, and administrators, who each contribute to its functioning by doing different bits and pieces, has begun to erode. Some go further, remarking the reforms in higher education amount to 'an assault on traditional academic values'.[26] Rodney Barker, who arrived at the School in 1971, notes that when he took up his post, 'finance was basically organised by one man', the 'Finance Officer'. Yet, increasingly, 'one feels that universities are a business run by a management, and the purpose of all these teachers and academics is to bring in funds'.[27] Echoing Barker, Nicholas Barr notes that the trajectory of academic life has been similar to tennis over the years.

---

[21] Ibid.
[22] Committee on Higher Education 1963: 90.
[23] Ibid.: 249.
[24] Hood telephone interview 2020.
[25] Frith 2019.
[26] Gewirtz & Cribb 2012: 69.
[27] Barker interview 2020.

Tennis turned professional, the strength, the quality of the game has increased immeasurably but something got lost as well ... We've become professionalised, productivity has increased enormously but something has got lost, including ... How many eccentrics are there at the LSE? There's not many ... I can remember the young Ken Binmore, the eminent mathematician and game theorist. As a young lecturer, he would be wandering around the School in bare feet because that's what he felt like doing ...[28]

The turn towards professionalisation sparked by both Brian Barry and Christopher Hood's leadership was, then, not without its flaws. Research and teaching standards increased, while student and staff members were better protected. Yet, something has also been lost along the way, something far harder to quantify. The Department began to feel more like a corporate enterprise, concerned with marketing, profits, image and future employment prospects. In such an environment, the eccentrics who used to dominate this community all but evaporated; a community that Oakeshott and others like him fought so hard to defend. Yet, despite concerns about the demise of academic life, the professionalisation of the Government Department was driven more by commercial and institutional factors than it was by the scholars themselves. Brian Barry and Christopher Hood merely managed to translate these wider, external pressures successfully into institutional reforms, laying the foundations for a different, but nevertheless promising, attitude to Politics at the LSE.

New Blood

Barry and Hood's approach to administration and hiring was a major reason for the LSE thriving in the early 2000s as a hub for political research. On the political science and public administration side, academics began to focus their work on comparative studies, particularly in European politics. Despite being remembered as a 'lively' research centre during the 1980s by Professor Patrick Dunleavy, the Department's European Group had been small before the 1990s.[29] While professors had taught on European states and thought since the School's founding, little effort had been made to turn this into the study of Europe and its emerging institutions under the Oakeshottian old guard. As Christopher Hood departed for All Souls College in 2001, this process was already underway.

The appointments made by the new, professionalised Department significantly expanded their European focus, beginning with the arrival of Klaus Goetz in 1992 from Nuffield College, Oxford. Simon Hix joined in 1997 from

---

[28] Barr interview 2020.
[29] Dunleavy interview 2019.

Brunel, focusing his research on institutions, voting and the politics of Europe. He would become a recognisable and influential voice over the next two decades, and in 2015 would assume the inaugural Harold Laski Chair in Political Science, in memory of the Department's famous wartime professor. Sara Hobolt, the current occupant of the Sutherland Chair in European Institutions, arrived from St. John's College, Cambridge, as another expert in European politics, centring her research on referendums and democratic politics. Both were key members of Hood's 'new contingent' who, alongside Keith Dowding, Mark Thatcher and Paul Mitchell, helped create a stronger European Comparative Politics group in the Department.[30] Mitchell, who was appointed in 2000 and arrived in 2001 from Harvard, lectured on European Politics and research methodology, with a particular focus on Irish elections. Brendan O'Leary took over from Hood as Convener that year, continuing the trend that had been developing since Barry. Torun Dewan joined the Department from Nuffield College, Oxford, in 2002, with a focus on the political economy of parties and coalitions. Together with Barry, Hood and Dunleavy, this group of political scientists set out a new vision for the discipline at the School.

This vision was driven by a series of institutes either founded or significantly influenced by the Department. The European Institute was set up in 1991 by Howard Machin and other Government faculty to study both political integration and fragmentation in Europe, running alongside the West German Group. These were followed in 2015 by the 'UK in a Changing Europe' institute, set up to improve UK/EU research access jointly between the European Social Research Council (ESRC) and King's College London. The institute has involved many Government Department faculty in its research agenda, which has only increased in relevance and importance since the 2016 Referendum, and the decision for the United Kingdom to leave the European Union. Although recent, the decision has impacted on the internal affairs of the Department and the School as a whole. Several leading academics in the School who often advised the British Government on EU matters, such as Sara Hagemann, were informed their advice would not be sought on matters relating to Brexit because they were not British citizens. Other government faculty, such as Michael Barzelay, went on to join other institutes within the School. Barzelay, who joined in 1995, would remain a public administration lecturer until joining the Interdisciplinary Institute of Management in 2001, later becoming a founding member of the Department of Management in 2006.

Attempts were made to formalise the shift towards European studies, aligned with a more rigorous approach to Political Science. In 2010, the European Political Science Association (EPSA) was established. This new association involved many academics working on quantitative Political Science within the Government Department, and with a focus on the quantitative work done in the Political Studies group. The annual conference intended to 'represent and promote

---

[30] Hood telephone interview 2020.

political science in Europe'.[31] Simon Hix explains that one of the goals of the EPSA conference was to bring European Political Science in line with and up to the standards of the American Political Science Association. A second event led by individuals in the Department to consolidate the quantitative work was the Political Science and Political Economy Research Seminar, set up in 2009.[32]

This increased focus on European politics occurred alongside the gradual disappearance of the lingering 'Imperialist' Public Administration legacy from the Department's early years. The rapid diversification of the student body between 1990 and 2010 helped accelerate this process, with more students arriving from Europe and fewer from the Commonwealth nations. This change was part of a larger drive for the LSE to become a 'European institution'.[33] And, as Brendan O'Leary neared the end of his Convenership in 2001, the Department had positioned itself to lead this effort, both in terms of the students and its academic focus on European comparative public policy. O'Leary notes that during this period there were even discussions about ending the LSE's reliance on government funding, making it independent and able to specialise on Masters' programmes focused globally, but particularly on Europe. As of the calendar year 1990–1991, students taking 'Government' as their special subject for the BSc (Econ.) were eligible for the European Erasmus exchange programme, with particular focus given to the School's partner institution in France, Sciences Po, Paris.[34]

Prizes also began to proliferate in the School during this time, with the Government Department introducing a variety of awards to honour the academic performances of outstanding students. Among these are the Harold Laski Scholarship, awarded to the second-year BSc Government student with the best performance in both their first- and second-year examinations; the Bassett Memorial Prize, given to the final-year student with the best performance in the BSc Government or BSc Government and History programmes; and the Department of Government Dissertation Prizes, honouring outstanding performances on Government course dissertations at both Bachelors and Masters levels. A new prize was launched in 2020 to mark the 42 years of teaching in the Department by Patrick Dunleavy. The Patrick Dunleavy Prize is awarded to the BSc student with the best dissertation or long essay on public policy or elections.

The hiring story was similar for political theory. The Department mustered a series of impressive appointments, beginning with the arrival of Paul Kelly in 1995, and Anne Phillips in 1999. Kelly, whose main influences included Hart, Barry and Bentham, was active in the mid-1990s in helping establish the *Polit-*

---

[31] European Political Science Association 2019.

[32] Hix interview 2020.

[33] O'Leary interview 2020.

[34] LSE 1990.

ical Studies Review journal, which was published first in 2003.[35] His study of Western Political Thought with David Boucher, *Political Thinkers: From Socrates to the Present* (2003), remains a detailed introduction to the subject. Phillips, who initially joined as Director of the School's Gender Institute, gradually moved to a joint appointment with the Government Department in 2004 (later becoming a sole appointment), with her research bringing together gender and politics. She is the Graham Wallas Chair of Political Science and leads the graduate course on 'Feminist Political Theory', writing influential works such as *The Politics of the Human* (2015). Cecile Fabre joined the cohort from Oxford at the turn of the millennium, teaching on general political concepts and the history of political thought, with Katrin Flikschuh following suit three years later, lecturing on the political philosophy of Immanuel Kant.[36] The famous liberal political philosopher and sceptic, John Gray, was an active member of the Government Department, writing a number of influential, if controversial, works, such as *Two Faces of Liberalism* (2000), *Straw Dogs* (2002) and *Heresies* (2004). More analytical appointments were made in the vein of Christian List, who joined as a lecturer in 2002 before assuming a dual professorship in the Political Science and Philosophy Departments five years later, followed by Kai Spiekermann in 2007, working on the epistemological foundations of democratic theory.

Fabre departed for Oxford in 2007, marking a turn in the Department's attitude towards political philosophy. Chandran Kukathas arrived as Professor in Political Theory as Fabre left, a post he would continue to hold as Head of Department from 2015 until his departure in 2019. A leading liberal thinker famous for original works on multiculturalism, such as *The Liberal Archipelago: A Theory of Diversity and Freedom* (2007), as well as his understanding of Friedrich Hayek, Kukathas would extend the Department's traditional focus, teaching modules on the 'Introduction to Political Theory', 'Twentieth Century European Liberal Thought' and 'Advanced Study of Key Political Thinkers'. Yet, an increasingly alternative and eclectic selection of political theorists were drawn to the School, from Lea Ypi's work on Marxist theory and critical thought to Leigh Jenco's focus on comparative and Chinese Political Philosophy.[37] Katrin Flikschuh also expanded her readings, examining how political concepts emerge in non-Western thought, particularly in African philosophy.

The political scientists retained their focus on expanding European programmes, driven by a succession of Conveners: Dominic Lieven (2001–2004), George Philip (2004–2007), Rodney Barker (2007–2009) and Paul Kelly (2009–2012). During this time, the term 'Convener' fell into disuse, with the post increasingly being referred to as the Head of the Department. By late 2007, this title was almost the exclusive term for the role throughout the School. The School also detached itself from the University of London framework in 2008,

---

[35] Kelly 2020.
[36] LSE 2004: 142, 143, 287; LSE 2019.
[37] Kukathas Skype interview 2020.

Figure 18: The LSE Department of Government, 2018; Credit: LSE Library.

which it had been a part of since it was first awarded degree-conferring powers in 1900, allowing the Department to award its own LSE degrees for the first time. Simon Hix took over as Head of Department from Paul Kelly in 2012, continuing the trends that Barry had set out in the early 1990s. Hix worked hard to cement this new 'positive political science' vision at the School. Appointed Pro-Director of the School's research in 2018, Hix continued teaching undergraduates the 'Introduction to Political Science' course, which he renamed and restructured from the previous 'Introduction to Politics' course to make it more empirical.[38] The quantitative and political economy groups in the Department were further bolstered by the arrival of David Soskice from Nuffield College, Oxford, in 2012. He continued to specialise in macroeconomic research, particularly inequality, democracy and the economics of advanced capitalist countries, driving this crucial subdivision of the Department's research.

One noticeable change in the appointments process during these transformative years was the diversity of candidates and the prominence of women in the Department. Women have a long history at the LSE, which unlike the ancient universities was open to both male and female applicants from its founding. The first female teachers arrived at the School in 1896 when Gertrude Tuckwell, later President of the Women's Trade Union League, appeared on the faculty

---

[38] Hix interview 2020.

list, giving six lectures on factory legislation. The following year, she was joined by Ellen McArthur and Lillian Knowles, both former students of Girton College, Cambridge, and members of the 'Steamboat Ladies': graduates of Oxford and Cambridge between 1904 and 1907 who were refused degrees by their home institutions on grounds of their gender.[39] They were advised to take steamboats to Trinity College, Dublin, and have their undergraduate qualifications conferred *ad eundem gradum*—'at the same degree'—instead. This practice had been common for teachers looking to transfer between universities, but who were not graduates of the college they arrived at themselves. The "political science" (broadly defined) faculty hosted both Beatrice Webb and Ada Wallas from its inception, and in 1921 Lillian Knowles became the LSE's first female professor, teaching economic history.[40] Several decades later, Shirley Letwin would become a prominent member of the 'Oakeshottian Right'. Janet Coleman (starting in 1987) became the first woman to achieve a professorship in the Government Department in 1994. She was elected a fellow of the Royal Historical Society in recognition of her work, and specialised in the history of medieval political thought, co-founding the *History of Political Thought* journal in 1980. Although sometimes a contentious figure, she was a 'very able scholar' whose seminars were 'extremely inspirational', admired by both colleagues and students alike.[41]

However, despite these notable exceptions, women in academic positions were far from the norm for quite some time. Throughout the Department's history, most of its female employees were secretaries rather than researchers or professors. The workplace culture was still that of an 'old boys club' well into the 1980s, where alcohol-based after-office-hours functions were common, and sexual affairs not uncommon. Perhaps the highest profile of these workplace affairs were associated with Michael Oakeshott, known to be charming and rather flirtatious even into his later years. His close friend and colleague at the School, Dr. Anne Bohm, joked that prior to arriving at the LSE he was refused the Mastership of Gonville and Caius College, Cambridge, because the faculty 'didn't want him seducing their wives'.[42] He would later be found bathing nude at Margate Beach with several women and arrested, requiring the Director of the School to go to the local jail and have him released.[43] These snippets of life in the higher departmental echelons paint a small part of a larger picture, revealing what the dominant university culture was at the time. Only with shifts in British educational policy—and the Department's professionalising trend—did

---

[39] Donnelly 2018a; Donnelly 2018b.
[40] Ibid.
[41] Hood telephone interview 2020; Phillips interview 2020; Matravers interview 2020.
[42] Franco & Marsh 2012: 32.
[43] Barr interview 2020.

women begin arriving in significant numbers and become competitors for academic positions.[44]

The new blood in the Department had a marked impact on its image, character, research profile and drive. A surge in appointments had given the political theorists a new, professional direction, moving away from the grand historical approach of the previous decades. The political scientists and public administration specialists reshaped their focus, expanding beyond the old colonial roots of the School to embrace a new, European view. For the first time in its history, women now played a prominent role in the teaching, not just the administration, of political science. The 'Department in limbo' had completed its metamorphosis, emerging an altogether different creature.

Moving House

Alongside this shift in the faculty and student composition, another less obvious influence has been the Department's location. Located in Aldwych, central London, between the Royal Courts of Justice and Westminster, the Department and School has always been well positioned as a centre for the study of politics and government. Christopher Hood and George Jones ran an influential seminar series with senior academics and civil servants, followed by a similar series about the implications of Brexit, run by Tony Travers and Kevin Featherstone.[45] Patrick Dunleavy also ran several capstone projects with the Bank of England, the Department of International Development and the Financial Conduct Authority which would have been 'impossible' without the proximate nature of the Department.[46]

Over the last few decades, the Department has moved within the School three times. Initially, the political scientists had no fixed location, and were dispersed throughout its buildings like the rest of the academic staff. This was in keeping with the founding ideals of the LSE, explored in Chapters 1 and 2: The School was to be a new form of interdisciplinary social science university, where subject and faculty boundaries were almost invisible. However, as departments began to establish themselves as internally autonomous units within the wider School, the political scientists made a gradual move to their first location, with many settling in King's and Lincoln's Chambers around the 1950s. The Department moved again in the summer of 2007 to the more modern Connaught House, remaining there until the autumn of 2019, when it took up its present residence on floors three and four of the new Centre Building. Each of these locations had a profound impact, on students and staff alike, and were often representative of the broader transformations in the School's development.

---

[44] O'Leary interview 2020.
[45] Travers interview 2020.
[46] Dunleavy interview 2019.

The original move to King's and Lincoln's Chambers came about rather gradually, with the political scientists coalescing on this location as the central hub of their activity within the wider School. The Department itself was not formally located in the buildings, but in the neighbouring East Building, which the School had acquired in 1930.[47] Back then, its facilities consisted of just a single room, and several rooms adjacent for teaching. The subsequent grouping in King's and Lincoln's grew out of a general attraction of like-minded scholars to the location of key figures, who had chosen to take offices in these spaces.[48] It was 'a loose collection of people in a primary organisation, called LSE, which was bigger and more significant' than any one Department. Famous figures such as Ken Minogue and Elie Kedourie did not even reside in the buildings. This decentralised, 'higgledy piggledy' structure persisted well into the 1990s and wouldn't truly disappear until the early 2000s.[49] Offices were often shared with other academics, although unlike the modern Centre Building where junior academics share workspaces, these could be with faculty from any other Department. As mentioned in Chapter 2, John Charvet spent his first year in 1965 cohabiting with a lawyer, which he saw as reinforcing the idea that the School was a 'united band of social scientists', so 'it didn't matter who you were next to'.[50] The Chambers were also rather run down, emblematic of the Department's informal ethos of 'high thinking in austere conditions' rather than 'making money' or 'changing the world'.[51] 'Intellectually rich but physically poor', one former student recalls.[52] Brendan O'Leary recalls much the same, describing King's Chambers as a near-derelict building in need of maintenance:

> The LSE at that time was a physical slum … The wallpaper was peeling off the wall, if there was wallpaper. It was damp. It was a health hazard. I put my hands once through a window and, as you can see, my fingers are no longer straight to this day. I broke a finger because I slipped on the staircase. Not because I was lacking sobriety but because the staircases were dangerous.

However, while the Department's first home required significant restoration, it also had a certain 'old-world charm', which made it quite popular with students.[53] Matt Matravers, who arrived in the Department as an undergraduate student in 1987, took his seminars on medieval political thought with Janet Coleman in King's Chambers, which he 'absolutely adored'. He recalls that there

---

[47] Alexander interview 2020.
[48] Kelly interview 2020.
[49] Charvet interview 2020.
[50] Ibid.
[51] Ibid.
[52] Alexander interview 2020.
[53] Hood telephone interview 2020.

were two pubs built into the Department, with the Shapiro room located on the first floor as a common room. They took seminars in Janet Coleman's office as there were only 12 students registered for her course.

> Janet would put on a filtered coffee machine that would bubble and then she would smoke cigarettes non-stop through the seminar. It was a two-hour seminar. So you sat in all crowded with the coffee maker bubbling and just Janet disappearing behind a wall of smoke after two hours when she just talked about the nature of the good ... If you were nineteen, it was everything you imagined for an intellectual life to be ... The whole thing just had a character.[54]

Others enjoyed the layout of the LSE precisely because it was nothing like a campus with centralised departments, but rather was seamlessly built into central London itself. Jane Headland, a student in the Department in the 1970s, says: 'There was traffic on the road that went through when I was here. You were just in some buildings that were in a corner of London. You didn't have the feeling of being cut off at all ... I'm a city person. I have to be part of my city.'

Yet, for all the Chambers' character and charm, they were not well suited to the demands of modern academic life. The buildings, which had both been founded in 1905, had short, narrow corridors and no means of disabled access. Their condition eventually became so poor that, during the Department's final months there, part of the ceiling of King's Chambers collapsed on Professor Christian List's head. Moreover, the idea of having faculty members dispersed across campus grew increasingly out of fashion, and the lack of disabled access made them increasingly untenable as a home for the political scientists. This, coupled with the Department's growth in size and student and staff demographics changing, meant the Chambers were no longer suitable as a home.

The task of finding a new location fell to Christopher Hood, who proposed a wholesale move from the Chambers to Connaught House during his Convenership. This relocation, which eventually took place under Rodney Barker in 2007, meant that the Government Department now formed part of the main hub of the school, with rooms looking out onto campus.[55] Connaught House, which was leased to the School in 1966 and purchased in 1989, gave the Department its first real, definitive home. However, for some faculty members, this presented a significant, and sometimes unwelcome, change. Rodney Barker recalls that many took issue with the glass walls of the corridors, which meant people could see into academics' offices. Some put up notices or posters to try and deter unwanted amounts of attention, preventing people from looking in. However, others 'clearly liked' that they were on permanent display, and 'those

---

[54] Matravers interview 2020.
[55] Barker interview 2020.

who wanted to be a bit more civilized about it put up orchids' instead.[56] The design of Connaught House also made it difficult to build a sense of community and to work together. 'There's lots of secret cut throughs to the Old Building', recall Carla Seesunker and Claire Tomlinson, meaning 'people got lost really easily'.[57] There was a 'great big stairlift in the middle' with the offices coming off the sides, meaning that 'you often didn't see people'.[58] As it was a difficult building to get to, often 'a lot of the students didn't know' where the Department was. A long-term solution materialised when the LSE permanently rehoused the Government Department in a new, purpose-built, state-of-the-art facility.

The move occurred in the autumn of 2019, when the School completed construction of the new Centre Building in the heart of the Aldwych campus. The building was a stark contrast to all previous locations, and was initially met with some criticism, especially regarding open office spaces and noise levels. However, the majority of students and staff quickly accepted the Centre Building as their new home. The space provided a more conducive working environment than Connaught House, encouraging and facilitating interaction and collaboration with its wide corridors and open spaces. Claire Tomlinson, the Undergraduate Programmes Administrator for the Government Department, comments:

> I felt a change in terms of how much more visible we are, but also how much more visible the students are. And actually, it is nice to see them … If there's a student you had a conversation on email with, it's nice to then see them later on … But we also, I think, see a lot more faculty.

Yet, despite the advantages the Centre Building undoubtedly brings, there remains a lingering feeling that something important has been lost from the School's old way of life. With its corporate feel and layout, the Centre Building perhaps represents the final stage in the commercialisation process of the Government Department, and higher education as a whole. In the words of one former alumnus, it's 'a totally different world'.[59] This is especially true for those who knew King's and Lincoln's Chambers intimately. Professor Matravers recalls that:

> In 1987 nothing at the LSE looked like a corporate business. The front entrance was covered with papers, the lifts never worked and a lot of teaching happened in the Old Building, so you would walk in and there were many people trying to wait for lifts or go up and down the stairs, there were posters everywhere. And I think I rather miss these days

---

[56] Ibid.
[57] Tomlinson & Seesunker interview 2020.
[58] Ibid.
[59] Headland interview 2020.

when university didn't feel like walking into KPMG and for that reason King's Chambers was a delight.[50]

Upon returning to the School, alumna Jane Headland feels similarly, comparing the Centre Building to the Chambers where she studied:

> I didn't know anywhere else in London that was like [the Government Department], whereas now it really could be anywhere in a modern city. At first glance, it really lost its very particular feel … I am beginning to sense that the modern spaces all look the same … I am not usually someone who prefers the past, but I think in this case I might do.[61]

The history of the Department's location since its inception, from its initial dispersal throughout the School to King's and Lincoln's Chambers, from the Chambers to Connaught House, and from Connaught to the Centre Building, gives the impression of a Department progressing over the years. Its historic, internal struggle between its different component parts—the Old Fabian public administration cohort and rational political scientists rubbing up against the more sceptical Oakeshottian theorists and historians—has played out within their walls. Yet, this touches on another side of the Department's history, one that is entangled in the story of the purpose of a university education. Each move brought the Department closer to its current iteration—perhaps the leading European centre for political science, within one of the foremost social science institutions in the world—yet, each stage also lost something in the process. A certain charm here, a certain eccentricity there, chipping away at the older essence of the School as a community of scholars. While it would be hard to claim this communal feeling has fully disappeared, the Department today projects quite a different image to that of its predecessors. One that has, like many institutions, sacrificed a measure of its character and charm for a more polished, corporate feel. This history of the Department's location is but the most outward and tangible representation of this change.

Conclusion: The Future of Political Science at the London School of Economics

The three decades since 1990 have seen some of the most significant changes in the makeup and structure of the Government Department since students first walked through its doors, some 125 years ago. Adapting to the demands of modern higher education, the Department reformulated itself as a leading centre of political science and public administration, drawing a diverse body of

---

[60] Matravers interview 2020.
[61] Headland interview 2020.

students and professors to study from around the world. A new, sharper focus on its strengths and aims restructured its academic specialisations, looking towards a new Europe and an empirical, scientific form of political analysis. Its strengths in theory and philosophy expanded to include new approaches and methodologies, complementing this quantitative drive.

Yet, this period also raises questions about both the nature and the practice of political science, and the idea of a university education itself. One of the most striking criticisms of the new character of the Department since the early 1990s has been the gradual disappearance of a certain informal scholarly atmosphere, replaced by a more sanitised, efficient, professional attitude to political science. This has not just been confined to the LSE, of course. Universities across both Britain and the wider world have experienced a similar event. A far higher number of students now attend university in the United Kingdom, with over 1.9 million attending in the academic year 2018–2019.[62] This has been accompanied by a five-fold increase in undergraduate degrees awarded since 1990 and steep grade inflation, with a rise in the proportion of Firsts from just 7% in 1994 to 29% in 2019. Masters' degrees are now almost 10 times as common as they used to be.[63] As a result, the professional quality and standard of education at top schools demands a certain rigour that departments must match to retain their prestige in the academic market—a factor that is influential in the new marketised world of higher education. The decline of 'the university' as scholar-run space, almost unconcerned with issues like managerialism, institutional image or branding, has gone hand in hand with this drive towards marketisation. A history of the Department sheds light on this internal struggle over the purpose of a university education in 'political science'. What does such an education entail? Should it be driven by explorations of philosophy and history, opening the mind of the student to the various 'languages' of a liberal education, and teaching them to be fluent in them? Or should it be geared towards the more practical, career-related challenges a student faces after university, focused on technical expertise and positive, empirical analysis. Does favouring one side necessarily sacrifice aspects of the other? These are the subtle questions that continue to be asked of political science—and indeed the social sciences as a whole—as they continue to evolve as disciplines. And, for the Department of Government itself, how best can it live up to the hopeful ideal its Founders set for it: to advance the ideals of the Fabians for the betterment of society?

As the Department looks forward to the 21st century, new challenges loom, both near and further out on the horizon. The practical consequences of Britain's withdrawal from the European Union, although not yet clear, could be 'extremely serious', posing a threat to the School as a whole.[64] The Department is well placed to provide expert opinions and research on the subject, which

[62] HESA n.d.
[63] Lambert 2019.
[64] O'Leary interview 2020.

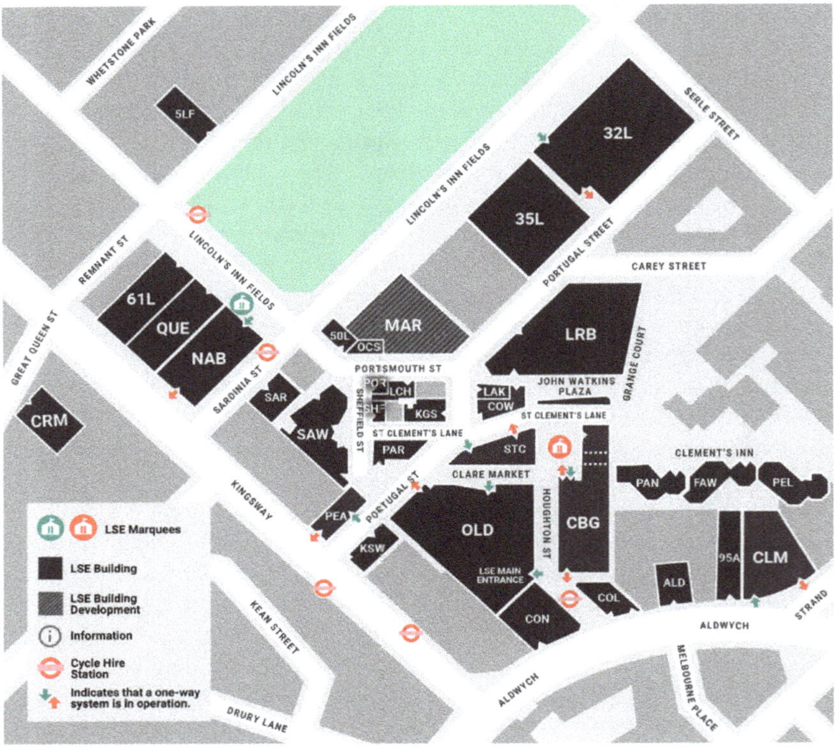

Figure 19: Map of the School, 2019–2020; Credit: LSE Library.

will likely define the next decade of British politics, yet its own future remains uncertain. While London will remain a focal point for international students, whether they can or will want to come after Brexit remains one of the Department's driving, long-term concerns. COVID-19, of course, poses new threats to higher education, driving learning and teaching into virtual spaces since emerging as an international crisis. It is too soon to predict how this pandemic will change the School as a whole, but early indications suggest that it is a challenge as great, if not greater, than that faced at the height of the Second World War. Atop these immediate concerns, the more lasting threat of climate change (e.g. restricting global travel) becomes keener with each new year, forcing itself into the long-term strategies of institutions like the LSE. These events, and the responses taken to them, will shape the future decades of the Department of Government in ways few can reliably predict.

Yet, amid all this uncertainty, there is good reason to believe the Department will not just survive these emergent issues but thrive while addressing them. As a world-class research institution, the LSE is perhaps better placed than other universities to help mitigate the impacts of these new and serious threats presented by the contemporary world. The School has faced serious challenges throughout its 125-year history, from the World Wars of the first half of the 20th century to the student riots of the late 1960s, while adapting well to the educational reforms of the last four decades. And, despite concerns, it has not just recovered from these challenges, but come back all the stronger having faced them, leading the development of political theory and political science along the way.

Appendix: Conveners and Heads of Department

- Harold Laski, informal head, 1921–1950
- Michael Oakeshott, 1962–66, informal head since 1950
- Harold R. G. Greaves, 1966–1969
- Leonard B. Shapiro, 1969–1972
- Peter J. O. Self, 1972–1975
- Elie. Kedourie, 1975–1978
- William Letwin, 1978–1981
- Maurice W. Cranston, 1981–1984
- George W. Jones, 1984–1987
- Kenneth Minogue, 1987–1990
- Gordon R. Smith, 1990–1993
- Brian Barry, 1993–1995
- Alan Beattie, 1995
- Christopher Hood, 1995–1998
- Brendan O'Leary, 1998–2001, first elected Convenor
- Dominic Lieven, 2001–2004
- George Philip, 2004–2007, title of Convenor still in use as of 2006
- Rodney Barker, 2007–2009
- Paul Kelly, 2009–2012
- Simon Hix, 2012–2015
- Chandran Kukathas, 2015–2019
- Cheryl Schonhardt-Bailey, 2019–2022

References

Broecke, S and **Hamed, J** 2008 Gender gaps in higher education participation: An analysis of the relationship between prior attainment and young participation by gender, socio-economic class and ethnicity, Department for Innovation, Universities and Skills Research Report, 08 14.

Committee on Higher Education 1963 *Higher education: Report of the Committee appointed by the Prime Minister under the Chairmanship of Lord Robbins 1961–63*, Cmnd. 2154, London, 23 September, 90.

Donnelly, S 2018a 24 LSE women in 1918. Available at https://blogs.lse.ac.uk
/lsehistory/2018/03/28/lse-women-1918/.

Donnelly, S 2018b Women at LSE 1895–1932—facts and figures. Available at
https://blogs.lse.ac.uk/lsehistory/2018/04/04/women-at-lse-1895–1932/.

European Political Science Association 2019 About EPSA. Available at
https://www.epsanet.org/about-epsa/.

Franco, P and **Marsh, L** 2012 *A companion to Michael Oakeshott.* University
Park, PA: Pennsylvania State University Press.

Frith, U 2019 Restrict researchers to one paper a year, says UCL professor,
THE World University Rankings. Available at https://www.timeshigheredu
cation.com/news/restrict-researchers-one-paper-ayear-says-ucl
-professor#:~:text=When%20many%20successful%20scientists
%20boast,appear%20to%20ring%20rather%20hollow.

Gewirtz, S and **Cribb, A** 2012 Representing 30 years of higher education
change: UK universities and the Times Higher. *Journal of Educational
Administration and History,* 45(1): 58–83.

HESA n.d. *HESA student record, 2018–19.* Available at https://www.hesa.ac.uk
/collection/c18051.

Kelly, P 2009 Brian Barry, *The Guardian,* 31 March. Available at https://www
.theguardian.com/books/2009/mar/31/brian-barry-philosophy.

Kelly, P 2020 Background of PSR. *Political Studies Review,* 7 April. Available at
https://psr.brunel.ac.uk/2020/04/07/bg-of-psr/.

Lambert, H 2019 The great university con: How the British degree lost its
value, *New Statesman,* 21 August.

Lieven, D 2001 *Empire: The Russian Empire and its rivals.* Yale, CT: Yale
University Press.

LSE 1987 *The London School of Economics and Political Science, University of
London, Calendar for the ninety-third session, 1987–88.* London: London
School of Economics and Political Science.

LSE 1988 *The London School of Economics and Political Science, University of
London, Calendar for the ninety-fourth session, 1988–1989.* London: London
School of Economics and Political Science.

LSE 1989 *The London School of Economics and Political Science, University of
London, Calendar for the ninety-fifth session, 1989–1990.* London: London
School of Economics and Political Science.

LSE 1990 *The London School of Economics and Political Science, University of
London, Calendar for the ninety-sixth session, 1990–1991.* London: London
School of Economics and Political Science.

LSE 2004 *The London School of Economics and Political Science, University
of London, Calendar for the one hundred and tenth session, 2004–2005.*
London: London School of Economics and Political Science.

LSE 2019 *The London School of Economics and Political Science, University of London, Calendar for the one hundred and twenty fifth session, 2019–2020.* London: London School of Economics and Political Science.

Weale, A 2010 Brian Michael Barry. *Proceedings of the British Academy*, 166, 3–23.

Interviews

Barker, Rodney, in-person interview by Hilke Gudel, 10 February 2020.

Barr, Nicholas, Zoom interview by Hilke Gudel, 16 April 2020.

Charvet, John, in-person interview by Sara Luxmoore, 18 February 2020.

Dowding, Keith, Zoom interview by Hilke Gudel, 25 April 2020.

Dunleavy, Patrick, in-person interview by Cheryl Schonhardt-Bailey, 6 December 2019.

Headland, Jane, in-person interview by Hilke Gudel, 20 February 2020.

Hix, Simon, in-person interview by Hilke Gudel, London, 13 February 2020.

Hood, Christopher, telephone interview by Hilke Gudel, 8 May 2020.

Kelly, Paul, in-person interview by Lukasz Kremky, 13 February 2020.

Kukathas, Chandran, Skype interview by Hilke Gudel, 11 February 2020.

Matravers, Matt, Zoom interview by Hilke Gudel, 22 May 2020.

O'Leary, Brendan, in-person interview by Hilke Gudel, 3 February 2020.

Phillips, Anne, telephone interview by Hilke Gudel, 23 March 2020.

Tomlinson, Claire and Seesunker, Carla, in-person interview by Sara Luxmoore, 26 February 2020.

Travers, Tony, interview by Hilke Gudel, 25 March 2020.

Weale, Albert, telephone interview by Hilke Gudel, 15 April 2020.

Withers, I. Zoom interview by Hilke Gudel, 29 May 2020.

Conclusion

An Insider's Perspective

Cheryl Schonhardt-Bailey

Where We Are Now

In autumn 2019, the idea for this history volume began. Funding was obtained and a team of researchers were recruited for the task of writing the first history of the LSE Government Department. We were confident that by looking backwards and tracing the origins of political science at the LSE, we would cement the importance of our discipline as fundamental to the very identity of the 'London School of Economics AND Political Science'. In so doing, we would also contribute to the enthusiasm surrounding the 125th anniversary of the School.

By January 2020, we had acquired some of the necessary archival material from the Library, interviews had begun, and the research effort was in full swing. Yet, by early February 2020, news was spreading fast of the new virus, COVID-19. Stories of catastrophic health crises from Wuhan, China, and then from the European continent began to radically shake LSE leadership. The prospect of a lockdown became less a question of 'if' and more one of 'when'. In the first 10 days of March, we were setting up Zoom accounts in the Government Department and preparing our 'business continuity' plan for working from

How to cite this book chapter:
Schonhardt-Bailey, C. 2021. Conclusion: An Insider's Perspective. In: Schonhardt-Bailey, C. and Bannerman, G. (eds.) *Political Science at the LSE: A History of the Department of Government, from the Webbs to COVID*. Pp. 137–154. London: Ubiquity Press. DOI: https://doi.org/10.5334/bcn.f. License: CC-BY-NC

Figure 20: Professor Tony Travers, lecturing outside during Welcome Week 2020, to observe COVID restrictions. Credit: James Robins.

home. On 10 March, LSE Director Minouche Shafik sent an email to all staff, noting that 'given the exceptional circumstances, LSE's position is to extend our current policy of not penalising students for non-attendance from three to four weeks, to cover the remainder of Lent Term'. But events moved rapidly. The next day, the SMC (School Management Committee) consulted with Heads of Departments about moving all teaching activity online. Discussion centred around whether we could pivot so quickly to make this happen within one week (16 March) or whether two weeks was needed. The SMC announced on 12 March that teaching would move online from 23 March (or before) and would remain online for the remainder of the academic year. All summer exams and assessments would also be delivered online and public events were suspended. While the campus and halls of residence would remain open, staff were encouraged to work from home. The pace of the crisis escalated so that by 22 March, the School had significantly scaled back its campus operations to about a dozen (mostly security) staff, thus resembling its typical closure arrangements over the Christmas holiday.

This was just the beginning of the disruption to follow for the remainder of 2020. Except for the School moving to Cambridge for six years during the Second World War, never had the School faced such an upheaval. With just weeks of planning, all examinations were given online. Summer School was cancelled entirely, and the School effectively became something of a ghost town over the summer months. Meanwhile, as international travel came to a standstill, academic and professional services staff continued to work throughout the summer in order to plan a 'return to campus' and some face-to-face teaching in autumn 2020, alongside the provision of all lectures online. Within the Department, individual members of staff were given 'risk assessments' to gauge whether they could 'safely' return to deliver face-to-face teaching. Heads of Department and Department Managers were faced with the daunting and uncomfortable task of assessing whether the pre-existing vulnerabilities of colleagues (health, age, home environment) posed a significant enough risk to warrant moving all their teaching online. Overall, the pandemic found its way into almost every aspect of the home and work lives of staff.

Perhaps one day a full history will be written on the impact of COVID-19 on the LSE. But this is not that day. Rather, my intention here is to provide some flavour for the backdrop of this concluding chapter. I find myself in a similar position to Ralf Dahrendorf, when he noted in his preface to *A History of the London School of Economics and Political Science, 1895–1995* that because he was 'an actor in the story which is told', he could not offer 'an impartial and objective account'.[1] As the current Head of the LSE Government Department and as someone who has been affiliated with the School since 1988,[2] I offer the same caveat. This concluding chapter thus follows Dahrendorf's lead in being written by one who is closely associated with the Government Department. Yet, unlike the chapters which precede this, the narrative in this concluding chapter also benefits from something of a 'social immersion' in the Department—or perhaps more informally (and for better or worse), an insider's view of the history of the Department over the past three decades, and including the tumultuous effect of COVID-19 on the LSE, and on the Government Department more specifically.

But, as part of this beginning to the end of the History volume, it is useful to observe, in brief, the basic components of the Department. As a snapshot of where we are now, the Government Department in 2020 is the academic home for 850 students (505 BSc, 305 MSc and 40 MRes/PhD). In the 2019–2020

---

[1] Dahrendorf 1995: vi–vii.

[2] As a UCLA PhD student, I was a visiting scholar in the Business History Unit in 1988. From 1989 to 1991, I was a Research Officer in the (former) Social Science and Administration Department, and then began my current employment in the Government Department from 1992.

academic year, 353 Government students were from the United Kingdom, but the rest came from no fewer than 79 other countries. The Government Department offers more BSc programmes than any other department in the School, with BScs in Politics, Politics and Economics, Politics and History, Politics and Philosophy, and Politics and International Relations. Together with eight MSc programmes, the teaching provision in the Department is among the most diverse of any department in the School. As for faculty, the Department has, in 2020, some 43 permanent academics, as well as 16 Fellows. In terms of sub-disciplinary strengths, the Department has six: Comparative Politics, Conflict Studies, Political Behaviour and Political Psychology, Political Economy and Institutional Analysis, Political Theory, and Public Policy and Public Administration. These numbers and lists are significant, as they capture a diverse, complex and at times unwieldy Department, and as such, will become relevant in the sections below.

And so, as we return to the three themes of this volume, the continuing effect of the pandemic is something of a prism through which these themes may be seen. In the Introduction, we set out three prominent themes for this history: (1) a transition from an era where one individual dominated the ethos, culture and direction of the Department to one in which it has become multifaceted—that is, a product of the visions and priorities of a number of scholars; (2) a periodisation within each chapter, which highlights dramatic events from each period (the birth of the LSE, the early imprints of Harold Laski and Michael Oakeshott, the 1960s protests and into Thatcherism, and finally the steady move towards professionalisation and into the COVID-19 global pandemic); and (3) the Government Department as a microcosm for significant developments in Britain (professionalisation of higher education, the centrality of London, the growing focus on Europe in the decades leading up to Brexit, and the issues pending for British higher education, post-Brexit, post-COVID). The following sections reflect upon each of these themes, in turn.

From One to Many

In both Chapters 1 and 2, we observed that a small number of prominent individuals were of fundamental importance in creating the vision and intellectual leadership for what later became the Government Department. We saw that three figures—Graham Wallas, Harold Laski and Michael Oakeshott—each, in his own way, had a vision for the 'political science' component of the School's two disciplinary pillars. But it was Beatrice Webb (as quoted in Chapter 1) who first seemed to recognise the core dilemma faced by these pioneers of political science. Lamenting in 1896 the 'wretched' candidates she was interviewing for Lecturer in Political Science, she wrote in her diary that it was 'a trifle difficult to teach a science which does not yet exist'. No doubt Wallas, Laski and most certainly Oakeshott all had some mental vision for the ideal collection of 'political science' (or, for Oakeshott, 'government') scholars. Oakeshott no doubt sought young academics whose outlook on the political and scholarly landscape resembled his own, and to some extent this drove his recruitment for the early Department. Such a strategy may have benefited from a single vision which could lend cohesion to a subset of politically minded scholars within the larger LSE community of scholars. And, it worked to some extent through to the middle part of the 20th century.

But, by the 1960s and certainly the 1970s, the Department had acquired a more diverse set of scholars, and the internal cleavage between Political Science and Public Administration became more apparent. As discussed in Chapters 3 and 4, the 'post-Oakeshottian divide' and then the pressures to professionalise both created tension within the Department, with silos emerging among scholars with different approaches to methodology and the direction of modern political science. Oakeshott's vision had given way to diversities in approaches and interpretations for what constituted 'political science'. Yet, even as late as 1995, Dahrendorf argued that 'modern political science' at the LSE had never even taken 'hold at the School, or in most British universities for that matter'.[3] Interpreting 'modern' as uniquely American, Dahrendorf maintained that none of the following three core elements of this approach was 'found to any significant extent at LSE': political analysis, political survey research and the 'economic analysis of politics'.[4] For Dahrendorf, modern political science had failed in Britain for reasons of substance and method: (1) the strength of traditional political philosophy; and (2) '[w]hen it comes to application, modern political science has turned out to be less effective than modern economic science'.[5] And so, by 1995, political science in the United Kingdom remained dominated by political theorists or political historians—at least, as viewed by Dahrendorf.

What Dahrendorf failed to capture in 1995 was that the Department had begun changing ('professionalising') from the last decade of the century (if not before), and with these changes came what Dahrendorf would characterise as modern (American) political science. As Chapter 4 describes, the arrival of Brian Barry to the Department in 1987 might be seen as a pivotal time in the move to 'modern political science'. Barry's arrival coincided with the convenorship (from 1987 to 1990) of a prominent Oakeshottian—Ken Minogue. The balance in the Department had shifted away from a focus on the history of political thought, although political history retained its supporters. For Barry, there was room for both, as seen in an anecdote from Anne Philipps. Before joining the Department, she had served as external examiner for political

---

[3] Dahrendorf 1995: 226–227.
[4] Ibid.: 227.
[5] Ibid.

theory courses in the Department, which entailed assessing the marking notes
from all the examiners:

> I was marking what must have been a first-year course, which was a
> kind of history of political thought course. Brian Barry had been drafted
> in as the second marker for this course, and he was notoriously dis-
> missive of the history of political thought. I mean, his view was: 'why
> on earth would you be in the slightest bit interested in what Plato said
> or in what Machiavelli said? What matters is having good, clear, strong
> arguments about the issues of today.' So, he had no interest in the his-
> tory of political thought, but he had to do this second marking. And I
> remember his marking comment for one of these undergraduate essays,
> which was on Machiavelli and which he gave a very generous 80% to,
> was 'sounds good to me, but what do I know?' Which always struck
> me as a very endearing illustration of both his dismissiveness and his
> willingness to accept that somebody might nonetheless be doing some
> very good work.[6]

So, whereas Barry was an undisputed force for modern political science, he
also accepted the multiplicity of approaches to the study of politics. From
Barry onwards, the Department acquired more of an embedded diversity of
perspectives on, and approaches to, political science. Over the next three decades, while professionalism transformed recruitment, teaching, administrative
structure and research, there was little in the way of a cohesive force within the
Department to alleviate the tendency towards (at times, fractious) silos. Indeed,
there were key features—namely the MSc programmes—which cemented fragmentation within the Department. From an era where the Department centred
around a single individual, the Department became one identified by a number
of scholars but dominated by no one. In some ways, this allowed a multidisci-
plinary array of research interests to grow, but it also made the management
of the Department tenuous at best, and certainly divisive at times. By the early
decades of the 21st century, the unresolved question in the Department was
where it was headed.

   In the decade following 2010, the Department continued to professionalise,
but staunchly resisted one rather managerial invention—namely that of the
strategic plan. When I assumed the role of Head in 2019, my one overriding task
(as given to me by the School's SMC) was to devise and implement the Department's first strategic plan. Whereas every other department in the School had
one, Government's failure to agree on a common future made this task seem-
ingly impossible. In early 2019, Michael Bruter, as Deputy Head of Department
for Research, drafted the Department's 'Research Strategy' document, which
was the first serious effort to summarise the research strengths and weak-
nesses of the Department. From his survey of colleagues in the Department,

---

[6] Phillips interview 2020.

Bruter found that we felt that individual scholarly talent and diversity in the Department were key strengths, but at the same time our main weakness was the 'energy we waste to cope with counter-productive divisions', along with 'intolerance' of others in the Department. Bruter pithily remarked: 'Strikingly … the main weakness of our Department is entirely of our own making.'

After about nine months of arduous work, and during Britain's first COVID lockdown, the Department approved its first Strategic Plan, in a contentious and anonymous electronic vote of 32 for, 7 against, and 4 abstaining. If anything represents the Department's solidification of 'modern political science', it can be found in its strategy. For one, the BSc in Politics and *History* was replaced with one in Politics and *Data Science*. Second, the silos created by the MSc programmes were unified in a single MSc in Political Science, with streams in Political Behaviour, Political Economy, Comparative/Conflict Politics and Global Politics. And, third, diversity among subdisciplines was formally recognised in the six research pillars of the Department (Comparative, Conflict, Political Behaviour and Political Psychology, Political Economy and Institutional Analysis, Political Theory and Philosophy, and Public Policy and Public Administration). Time will tell whether this plan will alleviate the 'main weakness of our Department'. In the meantime, completion of our Strategic Plan enabled us to move forward with clarity and focus to launch the largest single recruitment of new faculty—some six new assistant professors in 2021. Again, COVID dramatically shaped our processes as we conducted all the 26 'job talks', countless bilateral meetings with candidates, as well as deliberations and decision-making by Zoom. One could hardly imagine a more dramatic contrast from the 'old days' of recruitment, where a single pub conversation might yield a successful appointment.

Professionalisation and COVID-19

Each period covered by Chapters 1 through 4 highlighted at least one dramatic event or sequence of events, from the birth of the LSE and ending with the COVID-19 pandemic of 2020–2021. Rather than summarising these, my intention here is to focus on the last period, which falls squarely during my time in the Department. In Chapter 4, 'professionalisation of higher education' was the defining feature of the past three decades, and it is this professionalisation as well as the current period of COVID that is my focus here.

We saw in Chapter 4 a number of examples of professionalisation in the Department (reflected more broadly in other universities): more formalised recruitment practices; rigorous training for doctoral students; the commercialisation of higher education, as seen in extensive use of marketing, branding and managerialism; competition among universities, and the widespread use of rankings by research output (beginning in the 1980s with the Research Assessment Exercise and later becoming the Research Excellence Framework); and the shifting emphasis towards student satisfaction, predicated on the notion that students had become customers in the market for higher education. Others have described these trends in depth[7] (and some have also included the proliferation of awards and prizes for books, teachers, researchers, etc.), and argued that they have been spurred by broader 'massification and accountability pressures'.[8] Certainly, higher education is no different from other areas of the public sector which have seen an escalation in the pressures of accountability, at least since the late 1970s.[9] However, UK higher education has seen the added effect of a shift from 'effectively free' higher education from the 1960s to the 1990s, to one where undergraduates face fees of around £9,000 per annum, with post-graduates' fees ranging from about £15,000 to £25,000 or higher (in 2020). For some observers, this has meant that students are now 'customers exercising choice in paying for a product in a market' rather than 'citizens exercising a social right'[10] to higher education.

The most recent example of professionalisation, the Teaching Excellence Framework (TEF), builds on the university rankings model of the REF, but added to this the expectation that to inform their choices, students deserve a more transparent measure of the 'teaching quality' offered by universities. A fair amount of controversy has surrounded the TEF, and with the LSE receiving the lowest 'Bronze' award in the first TEF round (2017), the pressure was intense to find ways to improve our ranking. Given the close correlation between scores obtained on the National Student Survey (NSS) and the TEF award rank,[11] the most immediate way to improve was through the annual National Student Survey. From 2013 to 2020, the School's overall student satisfaction score took a significant dip, just at the time when national focus on the NSS and the TEF had grown. In 2013, the LSE's score of 88% was slightly above that of the sector average of 86%. However, between 2013 and 2018, the gap between the two widened considerably, as the School's satisfaction scores nosedived to 70.8%, while the sector's was 83.5%. Across the LSE and within the Department, significant changes in practices, resources and approaches all focused efforts on improving student satisfaction.[12]

---

[7] For an excellent historical overview of these trends as they pertain to British political science more broadly, see Grant 2010.

[8] Gewirtz & Cribb 2013: 80.

[9] Wright 2015.

[10] Anderson 2016.

[11] Bivariate correlations between three NSS metrics ('teaching on my course', 'assessment and feedback', 'academic support') are all over 0.95 (Department for Education 2017: 6).

[12] The 'elephant in the room' which many dismissed as a driving factor behind this large dip in satisfaction was, of course, the fact that the LSE campus had become a building site, as it demolished the old East Building, Anchorage and Clare Market, and replaced these with the new 13-storey, purpose-built Centre Building. It is no surprise that LSE student satisfaction in 2018 was

These efforts paid off in 2020—the LSE closed the gap in achieving an over-all satisfaction of 83.7%, with a sector average of 83%.[13] Perhaps ironically, in summer 2020, when the Government Department had much to celebrate in achieving a 10.2 percent increase in overall student satisfaction (to 82.6%) rela-tive to 2019, we were all working from home and frantically seeking to find ways to deliver some face-to-face teaching in the midst of the COVID pan-demic. Our considerable achievement in improving student satisfaction was unfortunately obscured by the overwhelming challenges we all faced in keeping our Department delivering high quality teaching in whatever ways we could (both online and in person, with COVID restrictions).

Whereas this may constitute a success story in the Department's long pro-gression towards professionalisation, it is important to recognise (as we did in Chapter 4) that professionalisation has not been an entirely welcome phe-nomenon in the Government Department. Certain features of the profession-alisation trend have created tension within the Department (e.g. marketing, managerialism, the pressures on publishing from the REF). But, it has been student satisfaction, both in student surveys (internal and with the NSS) and then culminating in the TEF, that have challenged colleagues to question fun-damentals, such as: What does it mean to be an academic at a 'research-led' university? How do we balance both the career- and REF-driven pressures to produce high-quality research, with the competing pressure to satisfy student demands for helpful feedback on assessments, the provision of a vibrant 'learn-ing community', well-organised courses and curriculums, and other criteria comprising student satisfaction? For some colleagues in the Department (and around the School), high-quality research and high-quality teaching were not necessarily compatible, or at least not in a sustainable way.

At the level of the Department, three features illustrate the increased focus on student satisfaction. First, the messaging from the School and within the Department helped to create a stronger culture of awareness of students as customers, who were paying hefty fees. Second, the Department had, by 2019, acquired the largest, most specialised team of administrators, in its Professional Services Staff (PSS). And so, positions such as 'Undergraduate Advisor', 'Com-munications and Events Manager' and 'Web and Digital Media Manager' now collaborated with management teams for both undergraduates and postgradu-ates to provide day-to-day (and longer-term) attention to the needs of students.

---

at its lowest, since the very students who completed the survey in this year had spent their entire undergraduate degree coping with the disruption, mess and unsightliness of the massive construction project. Undergradu-ate and postgraduate students graduating in 2018 had never even had the chance to walk down Houghton Street during their degree programmes.

[13] Coincidentally, the sparkling new Centre Building also opened its doors in time for the 2019–20 academic year, which may have influenced NSS scores for early spring 2020.

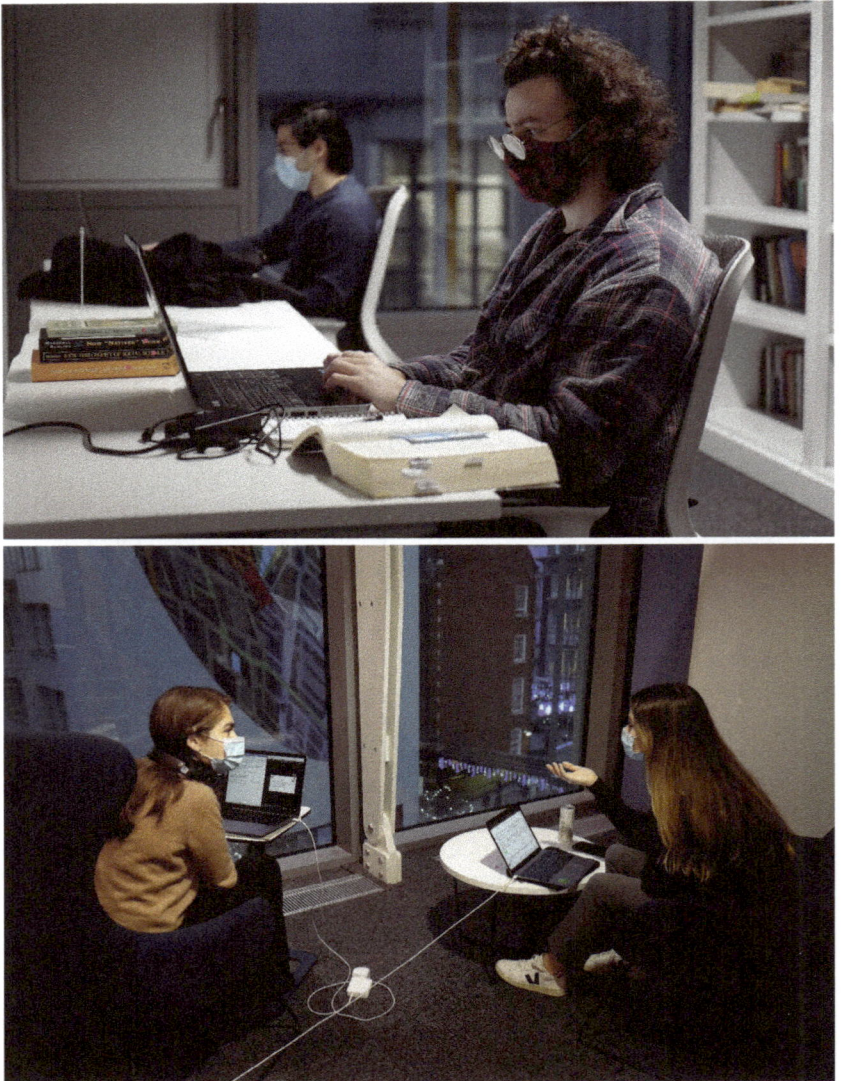

Figure 21: Government Department students during COVID (Centre Building). Credit: James Robins.

Third, the Department had, by 2019, acquired faculty positions in the form of 'Educational Career Track' (ECT) professorial lecturers (Paul Apostolidis[14]

---

[14] Associate Professorial Lecturer and Deputy Head of Department for Education.

and Vesselin Dimitrov[15]). Over the period of the School closure from COVID in the Lent term of 2020, through the summer and Michaelmas term in 2020, these three factors were pillars upon which the Department heavily relied during the upheaval of COVID. The commitment of faculty to sustaining high-quality teaching was perhaps most visible in the large array of short videos prepared by course instructors for our 'Welcome' website—certainly unprecedented among our faculty. As many MSc students were joining the Department from their homes in other countries around the world, these videos replaced normal 'taster' and introductory sessions. Additionally, the PSS team—many working from home—were specialised and trained to address the array of student needs, even under COVID. As we were alerted to students who either had tested positive with COVID or were forced to self-isolate, the PSS team kept close tabs on the welfare of these students. And, finally, the considerable logistical and pedagogical challenges in transforming lectures, seminars and classes to various formats (online, hybrid, face-to-face with masks and social distancing), and moving exams online were overseen by Apostolidis and Dimitrov. Despite the global pandemic, as well as previous years of internal divisions, the Department collectively 'pulled together' to ensure that, as far as possible, students were well-served in terms of their university education. If this sounds a little bit like boasting, it is. Even as some of my colleagues themselves fell ill with COVID, collectively we demonstrated a unity of purpose I would not have anticipated.

As a penultimate note to this section on the balancing of research and teaching, it would be remiss to not also mention the proactive stance of Government Department students themselves. Perhaps the most conspicuous example is the emergence of the LSE *Undergraduate Political Review*, or UPR, in 2015. This was the brainchild of a second-year student, Jack Winterton, who sought 'to create one of the best student-led publications on issues related to politics'. His idea was 'to create a student publication that [would not] replicate other journals, but rather try and find new ways to engage with discussions on the topic of politics'.[16] His motivation, and that of other students, was to establish a research-led platform for undergraduate research, which would share the research space of academics in the Department who sought to 'know the causes of things' (the LSE motto). The UPR (https://blogs.lse.ac.uk/lseupr/) hosts its own annual research conference, organises students into research teams to write publishable papers which they present at academic conferences, and publishes its own student research journal and blogs. With each new editor-in-chief,[17] the activities of the UPR have expanded. The emergence of the UPR serves as an organic and thriving example for how the passion for high-quality research (particularly

---

[15] Associate Professorial Lecturer.
[16] Winterton telephone interview 2020.
[17] Beginning with Winterton, these include Joshua Manby, Hannah Bailey, Karina Moxon, Adam Hudson and Jintao Zhu.

motivated from 'knowing the causes of things') can converge successfully with the 'learning environment'. I hesitate somewhat as I write this, for fear that it sounds too much like a 'sell'. It is not. I have personally watched the birth and growth of the UPR and have pondered its appeal among students. In my view, the appeal is that it allows students to identify with and be active participants in the research endeavours of professors. Commercialisation and professionalisation have not, at least in this example, dampened the intellectual curiosity in the real world of politics that also inspired Sidney and Beatrice Webb.

Lastly, we return to question the benefits from professionalisation. Certainly, not all my colleagues would agree that aspects of professionalisation—like the focus on marketing and branding, and the introduction of university league tables—have enhanced the scholarly environment that one hopes to find at universities. I have sympathy with these views. The memory of my early days in the Department—when my colleagues joined together for Wednesday lunches in the Senior Dining Room (complete with complimentary wine, which rather lessened my productivity for Wednesday afternoons), and personal interactions with colleagues and students featured more prominently than paper-trails—evokes something of a nostalgic feel. From the perspective of Government students from previous decades, we can also discern sentiments that highlight the unique intellectual rigour of the LSE in the late 20th century, along with its links to real-world politics. Michael Fougere remarks: 'I think in many ways the biggest thing I learned at the LSE was how to think, how to analyse, how to look at the world. Many of the questions I studied and issues I looked at still have an impact on how I see the world.'[18] Furthermore, Kennedy Stewart points to the 'exposure to international students, speakers, thinkers, diplomats ... and the intellectual rigour of the people you are surrounded with and the commitment to thought ... [I]t taught me how to think. It taught me to identify problems and to ask "why" questions, "why things happen," and that guides everything I do.'[19] As current mayors in Canada, both Fougere and Stewart epitomise the application of university education to governing and governments, as envisioned by the Webbs.

The question is, has professionalisation diminished the ability of the Department to evoke a sense of community among scholars or lessened the passion of students 'to understand the causes of things'? If 2020 has revealed one thing—both with experience of COVID and the completion of our first Strategic Plan—it is that the sense of community among colleagues in the Department is alive and well. Both in times of crisis and looking to the medium- to longer-term future, the Department retains both community and vision. And as for students? From the UPR, it is clear that some students are just as passionate as in decades past about pursuing the LSE motto. This has not diminished. What professionalisation has done, in my view, is to provide something of a safety net

---

[18] Fougere telephone interview 2020.
[19] Stewart telephone interview 2020.

for other students who might not conduct research as proactively or who might not foster a sense of curiosity about the causes of things. For students who may complete their LSE education with a simple sense of satisfaction that they received what their fees had purchased, professionalisation has no doubt lessened the scope for organisational/institutional failures by the Department or the School to have hampered their educational progress. Is this enough? In my view, it is.

But, more broadly, and as we have sought to explain, professionalisation has several dimensions. In one important respect, it is putting into practice the recognition that public institutions—of which universities form part—have to meet high standards of accountability and transparency (e.g., we have to explain to students why they obtain the marks that they do, rather than simply expecting them to take what is given at face value). Since, for the most part, political scientists are proponents of well-functioning public institutions, we can hardly excuse ourselves from this modern practice.

The Department as a Microcosm

Our third and final theme is that the Government Department represents something of a microcosm for significant developments in Britain (professionalisation of higher education, the centrality of London, the growing focus on Europe in the decades leading up to Brexit and the issues pending for British higher education, post-Brexit, post-COVID). Of these, my focus in this last theme is on the centrality of London, and the LSE situated in the heart of London.

As a broad generalisation, it is often said that the South East dominates the UK economically, politically, financially, and culturally. The independent, non-partisan Centre for Cities urban research unit gauges that 'the UK is by some measures the most geographically unequal developed economy in the world. While cities and large towns in the Greater South East of England are among the most productive and prosperous places in Europe, most in the North and Midlands lag far behind.'[20] The intention here is not to digress into a discussion of regional inequalities, but rather to note that London as an international city features prominently as a locus of economic, financial, political and cultural activity. As the LSE sits just a short distance from Parliament, the City of London, and the West End, it is not surprising that the geographic location of the LSE is a critical factor in its success. The following quotes each provide unique perspectives for the importance of London as home for the Department. First, Tim Besley, Professor in the LSE Economics Department, explains the significance of the LSE's home in the centre of London:

---

[20] Centre for Cities 2020.

… [W]e sit literally between the City of London and the City of Westminster. So … on the one hand you have the financial sector and on the other hand you have Government and we sit right between those two. So somehow, we are well positioned to capitalise on that. But in a more practical sense, you're based in London and there are other universities in London, so it's not just LSE. You can organise your day around [going to] … Westminster and be back at your desk [for the] afternoon. You can fill in your teaching around that, so it's a lot easier for those of us who are sitting in London to be fully immersed in the policy process in a way that it's not possible [for others] … But I think also, [and] I think this is very important about the LSE in general and the Government Department: the LSE also values that stuff. I mean, some places I can think of and particularly universities think you're not serious if you're too much engaged in policy, because you … should really be doing the more ivory tower style of research and I think it's sort of in the DNA of the LSE. And [in] the Government Department [it's] one of the elements or components of that DNA that we do support people who want to do their research in a way that allows them to engage in policy. We all take that for granted at LSE because we sort of assume it's true everywhere. But I can tell you, it's not. And that's a very important asset of LSE, and the Government Department has a key role in maintaining that asset.[21]

Similarly, Patrick Dunleavy comments on the fundamental importance of the Department being situated in the heart of London:

… I think that it would make a huge, huge difference [if we were not in London] because it's very, very handy to be proximate to the centres of power, particularly if you're doing political power or if you're doing parliament, public administration and public policy, parties, elections, and so on—all of which have been big areas for us over many years. I don't think we'd have had the same student body if we hadn't been in London, and we've had a very distinguished roster of people who've done their PhDs with us, some of whom are quite leading figures in the profession.[22]

As one of those 'distinguished PhDs'; former Shadow Chancellor of the Exchequer, Anneliese Dodds; remarks that, coming from Edinburgh, 'LSE was a great environment to be doing … comparative work, so I think it was mainly the draws of doing comparative social science that was the most attractive

---

[21] Besley telephone interview 2020.
[22] Dunleavy interview 2019.

[element] to me about being at LSE. I hadn't lived in London before, so that was kind of very, very exciting.'[23]

And, finally, from the perspective of an alumna who moved onto Oxford University from the LSE Government Department, Hannah Bailey notes that:

> ... having studied at Oxford, I can now say that it definitely doesn't compare in terms of the atmosphere. There is something about the LSE being in London, having the professors in the Government Department that it has, that really makes it in tune with the current political landscape in a way that I think other institutions aren't ... Even if you are not researching anything to do with the UK or London, just being in that hub really gives the LSE a particular buzz. I remember even one of my lectures was held in the Houses of Parliament with an MP talking to us about her work on a select committee. That was very exciting, and you don't get that anywhere else. We also had two election nights at the LSE. And it's really exciting being in the heart of London, reporters would come flocking in, we would all sit in the lecture theatre [as] we all waited in the projections at 10pm. It also gives you a lot of opportunities as a student. For example, I worked on an election night for ITV as part of an LSE scheme. I stayed up all night at ITV and we had people calling in for every constituency telling us the results for that constituency, and I had to type it into the computer, and it would pop up on the TV screen. That was so exciting. I really enjoyed that. I don't think you get these opportunities at other institutions outside of London.[24]

Without a doubt, much of the vibrancy of the LSE stems from its location in London and added to this is the institutional legacy of the Webbs and their followers to promote within university study the understanding of government, policy, and politics. As Besley notes above, engagement with policy is part of the 'DNA' of the LSE, and particularly the Government Department.

A corollary story of 'geography' is the movement of the Department from its island site in Lincoln's and King's Chambers to Connaught House in 2007 and then to the purpose-built Centre Building in 2019. The architecture of the Centre Building focused on creating collaborative space for 'learning environments' to thrive, for students to engage more with faculty and for social interactions to take place more organically both indoors, but also in a number of outdoor terraces and garden spaces. As a Department, we also hoped to use both the indoor and outdoor spaces to enhance our sense of community within the Department. Anne Phillips remarks that 'it's made a big difference in terms of a sense of staff and student engagement; just actually feeling part of the same community'. But she also notes that COVID has deprived us of taking

---

[23] Dodds telephone interview 2020.
[24] Bailey telephone interview 2020.

Figure 22: From King's Chambers (above) to the Centre Building (below). Credit: LSE Estates and Jean-Paul Meyer.

advantage of the open spaces in summer 2020, but anticipates that post-COVID, 'people will gather more on those balconies and that will also be a different kind of way of being at LSE'.[25]

The location of the Department itself from the antiquated, 'quaint' and wholly inadequate island site to the Centre Building provides something of a visual for the professionalisation discussed earlier. Marketing and branding associated with the architectural beauty of the Centre Building is far more attractive to prospective students than the depressing architecture of Lincoln's and King's Chambers, not to mention its dangerous stairwells, as noted in Chapter 4.[26] It is most definitely bittersweet that we had only months to enjoy our new home in the Centre Building before COVID hit, and sent us all working from home. However, working from home has transformed the image of our Department (and, for that matter, of academics throughout the world) beyond the physical infrastructure of our office and our building in London, to the small screens of our home computers. We are, individually, in 2020 (and into 2021) the Government Department in a new pixelised form, appearing through Zoom boxes in homes all over the world. Certainly, this has challenged us all in countless ways—from teaching to research to balancing pressures of family with those of working from home.

As a final comment, I will end with a multimedia example for how the Department has adapted to represent itself to the world. In the first COVID lockdown, as we had forfeited our geographic location in the new Centre Building and in London, we embarked upon an innovative way to convey the very spirit of policy-relevant research, in the form of multimedia content. Using Zoom interviews and VFX, we created a film in the style of 'dark Netflix' to inspire prospective students and to showcase the research that colleagues were already undertaking on the crisis of governments as they faced COVID-19—for instance, questioning the democratic limits to emergency powers during a pandemic, and how to gauge the success or failure of governments in saving lives as opposed to saving 'the economy' (https://youtu.be/U8JENWpppG4). Perhaps this is an example of marketing and professionalisation that traditionalists would eschew. But, for the Webbs, who sought to link theory with policy and action, our willingness to embrace whatever means necessary to be policy-relevant in a turbulent world would mark the best of the LSE tradition.

---

[25] Phillips interview 2020.

[26] My own story of these stairwells involves my husband, who, as he was carrying the pushchair of my son, slipped and fell down the stairs in King's Chambers. Thankfully, all survived intact.

References

Anderson, R 2016 University fees in historical perspective, *History and Policy*, February. Available at http://www.historyandpolicy.org/policy-papers/papers/university-fees-in-historical-perspective.
Centre for Cities 2020 Leveling up. Available at https://www.centreforcities.org/levelling-up/.
Dahrendorf, R 1995 *LSE: A history of the London School of Economics and Political Science, 1895–1995.* Oxford, Oxford University Press.
Department for Education 2017 *Teaching excellence and student outcomes framework: Analysis of metrics flags*, research report (DFE-RR736), London. Available at https://assets.publishing.service.gov.uk/government/uploads/system/uploads/attachment_data/file/651162/TEF-analysis_of_metrics_flags.pdf.
Gewirtz, S and **Cribb, A** 2013 Representing 30 years of higher education change: UK universities and the *Times Higher. Journal of Education Administration and History*, 45(1): 58–83.
Grant, W 2010 *The development of a discipline: The history of the political studies associate.* Chichester: Wiley-Blackwell.
Wright, T 2015 The politics of accountability. In: Ellio, M and Feldman, D (eds.), *The Cambridge companion to public law*. Cambridge, Cambridge University Press. pp. 96–115.

Interviews

Bailey, Hannah, telephone interview by Hilke Gudel, 27 March 2020.
Besley, Tim, telephone interview by Hilke Gudel, 24 April 2020.
Dodds, Anneliese, telephone interview by Hilke Gudel, 11 June 2020.
Dunleavy, Patrick, interview by Cheryl Schonhardt-Bailey, 6 December 2019.
Fougere, Michael, telephone interview by Hilke Gudel, 20 February 2020.
Phillips, Anne, interview by Hilke Gudel, 23 March 2020.
Stewart, Kennedy, telephone interview by Hilke Gudel, 24 January 2020.
Winterton, Jack, telephone interview by Hilke Gudel, 25 March 2020.

Interview Partners

Interview partners	Names	Relation with Department	Interview specifics
Alumni	Richard Alexander	BSc Government (1956–1959). Richard Alexander is retired. He acts as a trustee of the Flavel Centre, an arts organisation in Dartmouth.	17 February 2020. LSE campus. Interviewer: Hilke Gudel.
	Hannah Bailey	Hannah Bailey did her undergraduate degree in the LSE Government Department and is currently studying for a DPhil in Social Data Science at Oxford University. During her time at the LSE she was Editor of the *LSE Undergraduate Political Review*, an online platform that aims to promote undergraduate student research in political science.	27 March 2020. Telephone Interview. Interviewer: Hilke Gudel.
	Elly Chong	MSc Politics (1977). Elly Chong is currently retired. She returned to campus for a tour in December 2019. She is Emeriti Trustee at the Pacific University Oregon and acts as an President of Associated Chinese University Women.	5 February 2020. Telephone interview. Interviewer: Hilke Gudel.
	Anneliese Dodds MP	Anneliese Dodds is a Labour politician and former Shadow Chancellor of the Exchequer. She has served as an MP for Oxford East since 2017. Dodds completed her PhD degree in Government at the LSE. Period of affiliation with LSE: Completed PhD in Government in 2006.	11 June 2020. Telephone interview. Interviewer: Hilke Gudel.
	Michael W. Fougere	MSc Government (1979). Michael Fougere is an American-Canadian politician who is the current mayor of Regina, Saskatchewan. He was elected mayor in 2012. Prior to this, he served on various civic boards such as the Wascana Centre Authority, Sasketchewan Urban Municipalities Association, Tourism Regina and the Regina Downtown Business Improvement District.	20 February 2020. Telephone interview. Interviewer: Hilke Gudel.

(Contd.)

Interview Partners *(Continued)*

Interview partners	Names	Relation with Department	Interview specifics
	Jane Headland	Jane Headland worked in feature film finance and production for about 15 years, and is now retired. She did both her undergraduate and postgraduate degree in the LSE Government Department.	20 February 2020. LSE campus. Interviewer: Hilke Gudel.
	Jo Howey	BSc Government (1973–1976). Jo Howey had a career primarily in teaching. Later, she become involved in numerous boards as an independent non-political member. This included sitting on the Board of National Parks, Health and Derbyshire Police.	3 February 2020. LSE campus. Interviewer: Lukasz Kremky.
	Nader Ojjeh	MSc in Global Politics, (2013). Nader Ojjeh works at Monivest in Switzerland.	23 January 2020. LSE campus. Interviewer: Hilke Gudel.
	Kennedy Stewart	PhD in Government (2003). Kennedy Stewart is a Canadian politician and academic serving as the 40th and current mayor of Vancouver since 2018. As an academic, Stewart has published research on citizen participation, democratic reform and municipal reform.	24 January 2020. Telephone interview. Interviewer: Hilke Gudel.
	Jessica Templeton	MSc in Public Policy and Public Administration (2001), PhD (2012). Jessica Templeton is the Director of LSE 100, LSE's interdisciplinary course which is taken by all first- and second-year undergraduates. For her PhD, she looked at the role of science and scientists in global regulation of persistent organic pollutants.	2 April 2020. Telephone interview. Interviewer: Hilke Gudel.
	Jack Winterton	BSc Government (2016). He now works as a Student Adviser at LSE LIFE. His interests include student research, academic writing, art and politics, and promoting multidisciplinary curricula. During his studies, he founded the *LSE Undergraduate Political Review*, which is an online platform that aims to encourage and facilitate an engagement in high-level political research and the professional presentation of critical arguments by undergraduate students from universities around the world.	25 March 2020. Telephone interview. Interviewer: Hilke Gudel.

Interview Partners *(Continued)*

Interview partners	Names	Relation with Department	Interview specifics
Academics in Department	Professor Rodney Barker	Rodney Barker is Emeritus Professor of Government in the Government Department and Emeritus Professor of Rhetoric at Gresham College. He was also former Head of the Government Department. His work focuses on British politics, civil disobedience, legitimation, modern political ideologies, political identity, enmity, enemies, and political propaganda and rhetoric. Period of affiliation with the LSE: 1971–present: Staff.	10 February 2020. Rodney Barker's house. Interviewer: Hilke Gudel.
	Professor John Charvet	John Charvet is Emeritus Professor in Political Science in the Government Department. John's work focuses on liberalism, equality and human rights. Period of affiliation with the LSE: 1965–2003.	18 February 2020. LSE campus. Interviewer: Sara Luxmoore.
	Professor Patrick Dunleavy	Professor Patrick Dunleavy joined the LSE in 1979 as a Lecturer, was promoted to Reader in 1986 and Professor in 1989. He founded the LSE Public Policy Group in 1992, of which he became Co-Director of Democratic Audit and Chair. He became a founding member of the Academy of Social Sciences in 1999. Upon retirement from the Government Department in 2020, he became Editor of LSE Press. Period of affiliation with the LSE: 1979–continues: Staff.	6 December 2019. LSE campus. Interviewer: Professor Cheryl Schonhardt-Bailey.
	Professor Simon Hix	Simon is Pro-Director for Research and Harold Last Professor of Political science, as well as a previous Head in the Government Department. He is Fellow of the British Academy and Fellow of the Royal Society of Arts. His work focuses on democratic elections and institutions, voting and electoral system design, and EU institutions and politics. He is also Associate Editor of *European Union Politics* and founder and chairman of VoteWatch Europe. Simon is departing LSE for the European University Institute in late 2021. Period of affiliation with the LSE: 1987–1992: Student. 1997–2021: Staff.	13 February 2020. LSE campus. Interviewer: Hilke Gudel.

(Contd.)

Interview Partners *(Continued)*

Interview partners	Names	Relation with Department	Interview specifics
	Professor Christopher Hood	Christopher Hood was Professor of Public Administration and Public Policy in the Government Department until 2000. He also served as Head of Department. His work focuses on the study of executive government, regulation and public-sector reform. Period of affiliation with LSE: 1989–2000: Staff.	8 May 2020. Telephone interview. Interviewer: Hilke Gudel.
	Professor Paul Kelly	Paul Kelly is Professor of Political Philosophy in the Government Department and served as Head of Department, as well as a School Pro-Director. His work focuses on British Political Theory, Liberal Political Philosophy and Multiculturalism. Period of affiliation with the LSE: 1995–present: Staff.	13 February 2020. LSE campus. Interviewer: Lukasz Kremky.
	Professor Chandran Kukathas	Chandran Kukathas was Professor as well as Head of Government Department. He argues for a radically minimalist form of political liberalism, involving a plurality of legitimate forms of authority. Period of affiliation with the LSE: 2007–2019: Staff.	11 February 2020. Skype interview. Interviewer: Hilke Gudel.
	Professor Brendan O'Leary	Brendan O'Leary was Professor as well as Convenor of the Government Department. He has served as political and constitutional advisor to the United Nations, European Union and Kurdistan Regional Government of Iraq, as well as the UK and Irish Governments. Period of affiliation with the LSE: 1980—1983: PhD Student. 1983—2003: Staff.	3 February 2020. LSE campus. Interviewer: Hilke Gudel.
	Professor Anne Phillips	Anne Phillips is the Graham Wallas Professor of Political Science in the Department of Government and was the Director of the Gender Institute until 2004. She is a Fellow of the British Academy and Fellow of the Academy of Social Sciences. Anne engages with issues of democracy and representation; the relationship between equality and difference; the uneasy relationship between feminism and liberalism, feminism and multiculturalism; and the dangers of regarding the body as property. Period of affiliation with the LSE: 1999–present: Staff.	23 March 2020. Telephone interview. Interviewer: Hilke Gudel.

Interview Partners *(Continued)*

Interview partners	Names	Relation with Department	Interview specifics
	Professor Tony Travers	Tony Travers is a Visiting Professor in the LSE Government Department and Director of LSE London. His work focuses on local and regional government, elections and public service reform. Tony is chair of the British Government @ LSE research group and a regular guest on The HotSeat. Period of affiliation with LSE: 1987–present.	25 March 2020. Telephone interview. Interviewer: Hilke Gudel.
Professional Service Staff	Claire Tomlinson and Carla Seesunker	Carla is Undergraduate Programmes Manager. She manages undergraduate study, course choice, programme regulations, exams and assessments and student welfare. Claire was Undergraduate Administrator. She managed undergraduate Moodle and reading lists, undergraduate events, the Staff–Student Liaison Committee and undergraduate Research Internships. Period of affiliation with the LSE: Carla: 2015–present (Government Department), 10 years in total at the LSE. Claire: 2017–2020.	26 February 2020. LSE Campus. Interviewer: Sara Luxmoore.
	Imogen Withers	Imogen Withers was previously Communications Director for the Government Department, before becoming Director of Communications at LSE. She leads on internal communications and engagement. She focuses on improving the experiences of students and staff through delivering creative, impactful communications that maximise opportunities for dialogue, build community and support the School's strategic priorities. Period of affiliation with the LSE: 2013–present: Staff.	29 May 2020. Zoom interview. Interviewer: Hilke Gudel.
Academics outside the Department	Andrew Bailey	Andrew Bailey is Governor of the Bank of England. He is also husband to Cheryl Schonhardt-Bailey, current Head of the LSE Government Department. Bailey was briefly a research officer at the LSE in 1984, after completing his PhD at Queen's College, Cambridge, and before joining the Bank of England in 1985. He has since been a guest lecturer in the Government Department for the past 20 years and has previously helped in supervising undergraduate dissertations in the Department. Period of affiliation with the LSE: 1984–present: briefly as research officer and then as guest lecturer.	4 April 2020. Telephone interview. Interviewer: Hilke Gudel.

(Contd.)

Interview Partners *(Continued)*

Interview partners	Names	Relation with Department	Interview specifics
	Professor Nick Barr	Nicholas Barr is Professor of Public Economics at the LSE in the Department of Economics. His research focuses on the economic theory of the welfare state, social insurance, pensions, health finance and the finance of higher education. He has previously worked at the World Bank. Barr has done some teaching in the Government Department, and had a close professional partnership with Iain Crawford, a mature undergraduate student from the Government Department. Period of affiliation with the LSE: 1993–present: Professor of Public Economics.	16 April 2020. Zoom Interview. Interviewer: Hilke Gudel.
	Professor Sir Tim Besley	Tim Besley is School Professor of Economics of Political Science and W. Arthur Lewis Professor of Development Economics in the Department of Economics at the LSE. He served on the Bank of England's Monetary Policy Committee from 2006 to 2009, has been a member of the National Infrastructure Commission since 2015 and was President of the Econometric Society in 2018. Period of affiliation with the LSE: 1995–present: Professor in the Department of Economics.	24 April 2020. Telephone interview. Interviewer: Hilke Gudel.
	Lord Meghnad Desai	Lord Desai is a Labour politician and member of the British House of Lords. He is Emeritus Professor of Economics at the LSE, where he taught from 1965 to 2003. He taught econometrics, macroeconomics, Marxian economics and development economics. He was very active in the student protests. From 1990 to 1995, he served as the director and founding member of the LSE's Development Studies Institute. Period of affiliation with LSE: 1965–2003: Professor in the Department of Economics, former Director and founding member of LSE's Development Studies Institute.	7 May 2020. Telephone interview. Interviewer: Hilke Gudel.

Interview Partners *(Continued)*

Interview partners	Names	Relation with Department	Interview specifics
	Professor Keith Dowding	Keith Dowding is Professor of Political Science in Research School of Social Sciences at the Australian National University (ANU). He was previously Professor of Political Science at the LSE in the Government Department. Period of affiliation with LSE: 1992–2007: Member of Government Department faculty and Professor of Political Science.	25 April 2020. Zoom interview. Interviewer: Hilke Gudel.
	Professor Anthony Howe	Anthony Howe is Professor of Modern History at the University of East Anglia. He previously taught at the Department of International History at the LSE and Modern History at Oriel College, Oxford. Period of affiliation with LSE: 1983–2003.	11 May 2020. Telephone interview. Interviewer: Hilke Gudel.
	Professor Matt Matravers	Matt Matravers is Professor of Law at the University of York, having previously served as Professor of Politics and the Director of the School of Politics, Economics and Philosophy at the University of York. He is currently the Director of the Morell Centre for Toleration. He was affiliated with the LSE Government Department as an undergraduate student and then as a PhD student in political philosophy. Period of affiliation with LSE: 1987–1994: Undergraduate and then PhD student in the Government Department.	22 May 2020. Zoom interview. Interviewer: Hilke Gudel.
	Professor Albert Weale	Albert Weale is a country member associate of the Department, occasionally turning up over the last 40 years in the role of, *inter alia*, chair assessor, guest speaker, attender of workshops run by Brian Barry and external examiner of PhDs.	15 April 2020. Telephone interview. Interviewer: Hilke Gudel.
Other	LSE Undergraduate Political Review– –Student Discussion	The LSE Undergraduate Political Review is an online platform that aims to encourage and facilitate an engagement in high-level political research and the professional presentation of critical arguments by undergraduate students from universities around the world.	5 February 2020. LSE campus. Interviewer/ Host: Sara Luxmoore.

Index